Nine Lives

Copyright © 2000 by Westview Press, A Member of the Perseus Books Group

Published in 2000 in the United States of America by Westview Press, 5500 Central Avenue, Boulder, Colorado 80301-2877, and in the United Kingdom by Westview Press, 12 Hid's Copse Road, Cumnor Hill, Oxford OX2 9JJ

Find us on the World Wide Web at www.westviewpress.com

Library of Congress Cataloging-in-Publication Data
Messerschmidt, James W.
    Nine lives : adolescent masculinities, the body, and violence / James W. Messerschmidt.
        p.   cm.
    Includes bibliographical references and index.
    ISBN 0-8133-6666-6 (hc.)—ISBN 0-8133-6667-4 (pbk.)
    1. Crime—United States—Sex differences.   2. Violence—United States—Sex differences.
3. Masculinity—United States.   4. Criminal behavior—United States.   5. Teenage
boys—United States—Psychology—Case studies.   6.Teenage boys—United States—Social
conditions—Case studies.   I. Title.

HV6158 .M47   2000
364.36'0973—dc21   99-045726

The paper used in this publication meets the requirements of the American National Standard for Permanence of Paper for Printed Library Materials Z39.48-1984.

10   9   8   7   6   5   4   3   2   1

For Erik and Jan
two of the sweetest boys in the world

Contents

Acknowledgments

I am forever deeply grateful to Sam, John, Zack, Hugh, Perry, Lenny, Jerry, Dennis, and Alan for talking openly with me and sharing their lives—they are the core of this book. Without the cooperation of these nine boys, as well as their parents or guardians, this book would have never been written.

A number of people devoted much time and energy to the editing process. I am particularly indebted to Gray Cavender, Kim Cook, Karen Heimer, Nancy Jurik, Michael Kimmel, Bob Miller, Don Sabo, and Chrisona Schmidt, who read the entire manuscript and contributed important comments, criticisms, and editorial suggestions. Numerous people also commented on specific portions of the book at various stages of its development: Piers Beirne, Bob Connell, Sarah Fenstermaker, David Finkelhor, and Tony Jefferson. I thank all of these people for sharing their thoughts and ideas.

Access to the boys interviewed for this project was made possible by a number of people who graciously took time away from their own work to help me. Special thanks to Todd Cabelka and members of the University of Southern Maine Clinical Research Review Committee, Virginia Doss, Michael Graff, Tracy Morton, Sheila McKinley, Steve Muslawski, and Daniel Nee.

As always, the Access and Interlibrary Loan Services librarians at the University of Southern Maine's Glickman Family Library have been an essential component to my research. I thank in particular Cassandra Fitzherbert, Carr Ross, Barbara Stevens, and David Vardeman for their crucial assistance.

I owe considerable thanks to two editors at Westview Press—Adina Popescu and Andy Day—for their continued interest in and support of this project. I also wish to extend much appreciation to the entire staff at Westview Press, but especially Lisa Wigutoff, who served as project editor, and Tom Kulesa, for his work on the book cover.

Most of all, thanks to Ulla, Jan, and Erik for their everlasting love, strength, and encouragement.

Finally, parts of this book have appeared elsewhere in a different form. I thank Sage Publications for permission to reproduce the following: Chapters 2, 3, and 4 are revised and expanded versions of "Making Bodies Matter: Adolescent Masculinities, the Body, and Varieties of Violence," *Theoretical Criminology* 3, no. 2 (1999): 197–220.

James W. Messerschmidt

1
Introduction

On February 2, 1996, in Moses Lake, Washington, Barry Loukaitus (age 14) shot and killed a teacher and two students at his junior high school. In the past he had frequently been bullied by "jocks" in his school. Eight months later in Pearl, Mississippi, Luke Woodham (age 16) shot and killed two students in his high school. His girlfriend had recently broken up with him and he was consistently called "pudgy" and "gay" at school. Two months later in West Paducah, Kentucky, Michael Carneal (age 14) shot and killed three students in his high school. He had often been bullied at school and had been labeled "gay" in his school newspaper. On March 24, 1998, in Jonesboro, Arkansas, Mitchell Johnson (age 13) and accomplice Andrew Golden (age 11) shot and killed a teacher and four students in their junior high school. Both boys had been rejected by girls and Johnson was repeatedly bullied for being "fat." And on April 20, 1999, in Littleton, Colorado, Eric Harris (age 18) and Dylan Klebold (age 17) shot and killed a teacher, twelve students, and themselves. They had been routinely bullied by "jocks," labeled the "Trench Coat Mafia" by the same bullies, and called numerous degrading names, including "faggot." As the country attempts to make sense of these "school shootings" at the close of the millennium, the media pundits concentrate our attention on whether the cause is violent Internet games or easy access to firearms. Both are important subjects for discussion, but lost in the squabble is the fact that *all* of the school shooters are *boys* and that such violence might therefore have something to do with masculinity. Indeed, the mass media has all but ignored gender and its relationship to these shootings.

However, within the discipline of criminology there has emerged a new and growing interest in the relationship between masculinities and crime. Since the early 1990s, numerous works have been published, from individually authored books (Collier 1998; Messerschmidt 1993, 1997; Polk 1994) to edited volumes (Bowker 1998; Newburn and Stanko 1994)

1

to special issues of academic journals (Carlen and Jefferson 1996). This is not the first time criminologists have been interested in masculinity and its relation to crime. Such luminaries as Edwin Sutherland and Albert Cohen can be credited with actually placing masculinity on the criminological agenda by perceiving the theoretical importance of the gendered nature of crime. Yet these criminologists understood gender through a biologically based sex-role theory, the weaknesses of which are now well understood: It provides no grasp of gendered power, human agency, or the varieties of masculinities and femininities constructed historically, cross-culturally, in a given society, and throughout the life course (Connell 1987). Moreover, the social and historical context in which Sutherland and Cohen wrote embodied a relative absence of feminist theorizing and politics, and a presumed natural difference between women and men (Messerschmidt 1993).

The social situation today, however, is dramatically different. Second-wave feminism—originating in the 1960s—challenged the masculinist nature of the academy by illuminating the patterns of gendered power that social theory had all but ignored. In particular, feminism secured a permanent role for sexual politics in popular culture and moved analysis of gendered power to the forefront of much social thought. Moreover, feminist research—within and without criminology—spotlighted the nature and pervasiveness of violence against women. Since the mid-1970s feminist scholars have examined girls' and women's crime, the social control of girls and women, and women working in the criminal justice system (Daly and Chesney-Lind 1988; Naffine 1995). The importance of this feminist work is enormous. It has contributed significantly to the discipline of criminology and has made a lasting impact. Not only is the importance of gender to understanding crime more broadly acknowledged within the discipline, but it has led, logically, to the critical study of masculinity and crime. Boys and men are no longer seen as the "normal subjects"; rather, the social construction of masculinities has come under careful criminological scrutiny.

Feminism has exerted a major impact on my own life personally and as an academic and has led to concentrating my work on masculinities and crime. Two issues were critical in my decision. First, as my mentor and friend Bob Connell taught me, when we think about gender in terms of power relations, it becomes necessary to study the powerful (men) because, as with any structure of power and inequality (such as race and class), it matters to study the powerful. This is particularly important if we are committed to constructing a more equal society. Indeed, we must examine the advantaged, analyze how they act to reproduce that advantage, and probe what interest they may have in changing. Thus one reason for studying differences among men and diverse masculinities is to promote possibilities for change.

Additionally, the gendered practices of men and boys raise significant questions about crime. Men and boys dominate crime. Arrest, self-report, and victimization data reflect that men and boys perpetrate more conventional crimes and the more serious of these crimes than do women and girls. Moreover, men have a virtual monopoly on the commission of syndicated, corporate, and political crime. Indeed, gender has been advanced consistently by criminologists as the strongest predictor of criminal involvement. Consequently, studying masculinities gives us insights into understanding the highly gendered ratio of crime in industrialized societies as well as such national tragedies as the recent school shootings.

One particular form of crime related to masculinity is, of course, interpersonal violence. In June 1993, the American Sociological Association (ASA) convened an intensive workshop composed of leading sociologists working on violence. The goals of the workshop were to examine existing research on the social causes of violence, to identify promising research directions, and to address policy issues. Three years later the ASA published a workshop report, *Social Causes of Violence: Crafting a Science Agenda*, highlighting the nature of research conducted thus far on violence and identifying priority areas for future study. In particular, the report (Levine and Rosich 1996, 9) emphasizes that U.S. teenagers "have increasingly become both victims and perpetrators of violent crime" and that youth violence "is growing more rapidly than any other subgroup." Accordingly, the workshop report calls for research on the relationships among age, gender, social class, and violence, and it suggests that future studies should examine different forms of violence and how "situational or lifestyle factors" relate to them.

The bulk of previous criminological studies on teenage criminal violence concentrates on assault and homicide, usually within the context of "a gang" (see Short 1997 for a review). One form of youth violence overlooked in past criminological studies is adolescent male sexual violence. Until recently, social scientists paid scant attention to sexual offenses committed by teenage boys. Yet the seriousness of adolescent male sexual violence is reflected in adult patterns of sexual offenses that often begin in adolescence. For example, approximately 25 percent of adult male sex offenders report that their first sexual offense occurred during adolescence (Ryan 1997). Moreover, a significant proportion of all male sexual offenses are committed by persons under the age of eighteen. Approximately 25 percent of all rapes and 50 percent of all known cases of child sexual abuse can be attributed to adolescent male sex offenders (Davis and Leitenberg 1987; Fehrenbach et al. 1986; Ryan 1997). For these reasons—combined with the serious emotional and physical trauma levied against victims of sexual violence—there is a genuine need for extensive research on adolescent male sex offenders. Accordingly, the present work began as a research project on adolescent male sexual violence; investigation of this topic revealed that past research concentrated on identifying and describing characteristics that *may* be associated with adolescent male sexual violence. For example, the majority of offenders frequently (1) victimize girl acquaintances who are several years younger, (2) come from "dysfunctional families" (e.g., physically violent families), and (3) display problems with peer relationships (Ryan 1997).

My reading of the literature on adolescent male sex offenders additionally reveals that it remains unclear how, and to what extent, these dynamics actually influence the development of adolescent male sexual violence. Casual relationships are difficult to establish because of possible mediating factors not yet identified, possible variable interaction among characteristics already identified, and other variables as to how each characteristic may or may not contribute to specific type(s) of sexual violence. For example, as noted earlier, adolescent male sex offenders frequently are members of families in which physical and/or sexual abuse is present. Yet this fact alone provides scant information on its relationship with the ultimate sexual offending. In other words, simple correlation does not merit causal influence. Indeed, criminology has little to say about how boys from violent and nonviolent homes differ in personal trajectory. Furthermore, many more girls than boys are sexually victimized in the family, yet the vast majority of adolescent sex offenders are male. Thus past studies fail to explore how such sexual abuse and other "dysfunctional" family characteristics may or may not influence eventual offending. Indeed, as Pierce and Pierce (1990, 102) observe, it is difficult to determine if family dysfunction is the result of adolescent male sexual offending or if adolescent male sexual offending is a response to family dysfunction.

The identified gender of the vast majority of adolescent sex offenders triggers a second major concern with earlier research: Because studies of adolescent male sexual violence are appallingly gender blind, *no research considers the impact of gender on these boys.* Thus historically the gendered adolescent male sex offender has been missing from this research and therefore earlier studies did not consider the important relationship between the social construction of masculinity and adolescent sexual violence.

Third, past research seldom used matched comparison groups (e.g., nonviolent adolescent males with similar demographic characteristics). For example, why do some boys engage in sexual violence while other boys do not? More specifically, what are the similarities and differences between boys reared in physically violent families who become sex offenders and boys raised in physically nonviolent families who also become sex offenders? Without appropriate comparison it is difficult to determine whether family violence (physical, sexual, and verbal) is linked to adolescent male sexual violence. Indeed, this problem led Michael O'Brien (1991, 91) to conclude that comparing adolescent male sex offenders to other violent and nonviolent adolescents "would be interesting in that characteristics unique to sexual offenders might be discovered" and thus "remains an important research direction for the future."

This is precisely what I do in this study. Following the suggestions of Levine and Rosich and O'Brien, I compare working-class adolescent male *sex offenders* with a group of working-class *assaultive* boys and a group of working-class *nonviolent* boys.

Arguably, examination of adolescent offender experience may help explain and clarify certain research concerns on both types of violence and nonviolence by teenage boys. Accordingly, I have attempted to walk in the shoes of these boys—talk to them in depth about their experiences— and learn what they actually did and experienced in their lives that resulted in sexual or assaultive violence, or nonviolence. Shockingly, prior to this study there was neither information nor empirical research on the agency of the offender or on how such agency relates to the earlier identified characteristics.[1] However, to conceptualize the relationship among agency, gender, adolescence, and violence, it is critical to appreciate how adolescent male violent offenders construct and make sense of their particular world, and to comprehend the ways in which they interpret their own lives and the world around them. Realistically, how can we begin to understand adolescent male violence if we do not understand what it means to the offender himself?

The present study, then, seeks to understand certain boys' use of sexual or assaultive violence as a masculine practice. The chief questions of the study are: Why is it that some boys engage in violence and some boys do not? And why do the boys who engage in violence commit different types of violence? This differential use of violence is examined as a resource for "doing masculinity" in certain situations and under specific circumstances. To comprehend what it is about adolescent boys that motivates some to commit violence and some not, and why those who commit violence engage in different types (sexual versus assaultive), we must comprehend the social construction of masculinity—how sexual and/or assaultive violence may be a meaningful gendered construct and practice in itself. To understand adolescent male violence, we must bring active-gendered subjects solidly into the research picture.

Although none of the boys in the present study were involved in school shootings, their life stories and the social processes surrounding their violence is relevant to understanding the school killings from Moses Lake, Washington, to Littleton, Colorado. Like the boys involved in that specific type of adolescent male violence, the sexual and assaultive boys in this study are often the victims and/or perpetrators of peer abuse[2] and are deeply concerned about sexuality and relationships with girls.

However, before examining the specific nine lives in the study, let us look closely at the distinctive components of the theoretical framework guiding the research process and the methodology used to gather the data.

Structured Action Theory

Reflecting various theoretical origins (Giddens 1976, 1984; Connell 1987, 1995; West and Zimmerman 1987; West and Fenstermaker 1995), structured action theory emphasizes the construction of gender as a situated social and interactional accomplishment. In other words, gender grows out of social practices in specific social structural settings and serves to inform such practices in reciprocal relation.[3] Historical and social conditions shape the character and definition of sex categories (social identification of birth classification). Sex category and its meaning are given concrete expression by the specific social relations and historical context in which they are embedded. Moreover, in specific social situations we engage consistently in sex attribution—identifying and categorizing people by appropriate sex category while simultaneously categorizing ourselves to others (West and Fenstermaker 1995).

Nevertheless, as West and Fenstermaker (1995) argue, "doing gender" entails considerably more than the "social emblems" of sex category.

Rather, the social construction of gender involves a situated social and interactional accomplishment. Again, gender grows out of social practices in specific settings and serves to inform such practices in reciprocal relation. Although sex category defines social identification, "doing gender" (West and Zimmerman 1987) systematically corroborates that identification through social interaction. In effect, there is a plurality of forms in which gender is constructed: We coordinate our activities to "do" gender in situational ways.

Crucial to conceptualizing gender as a situated accomplishment is the notion of "accountability" (West and Zimmerman 1987). Because individuals realize that their behavior may be held accountable to others, they configure and orchestrate their actions in relation to how such action may be interpreted by others in the particular social context in which it occurs. In other words, in their daily activities individuals attempt to be identified socially as "female" or "male." In this way, accountability "allows individuals to conduct their activities in relation to their circumstances" (West and Fenstermaker 1995, 156), suggesting that gender varies by social situation and circumstance. Within social interaction, then, we encourage and expect others to attribute a particular sex category to us. And we facilitate the ongoing task of accountability through demonstrating that we are male or female by means of concocted behaviors that may be interpreted accordingly. Consequently, we do gender differently, depending on the social situation and the social circumstances we encounter. The particular meanings of gender are defined in social interaction and therefore through personal practice. "Doing gender" renders social action accountable in terms of normative conceptions, attitudes, and activities appropriate to one's sex category in the specific social situation in which one acts (West and Fenstermaker 1995).

In this view, then, gender is accomplished systematically—not imposed on people or settled beforehand—and is never a static or a finished product. Rather, people construct gender in specific social situations. In other words, people participate in self-regulating conduct whereby they monitor their own and others' social actions.

Relations, Structures, and Action

Although gender is "made," so to speak, through the unification of self-regulated practices, these practices do not occur in a vacuum. Instead, they are influenced by the social structural constraints we experience. Social structures, defined here as regular and patterned forms of interaction over time that constrain and channel behavior in specific ways, "only exist as the reproduced conduct of situated actors" (Giddens 1976, 127). As Connell (1987, 1995) argues, gendered social structures (e.g., divisions of labor, relations of power, and sexuality) are neither external to social actors nor simply and solely constraining. On the contrary, structure is realized only through social action, and social action requires structure as its condition. "Knowledgeable" human agents (people who know what they are doing and how to do it) enact social structures; agents put into practice their structured knowledge (Giddens 1984). Moreover, in certain circumstances, agents improvise or innovate in structurally shaped ways that significantly reconfigure the very structures that shaped them (Giddens 1984). Because people do gender in specific social situations, they reproduce and sometimes change social structures. And given that people reproduce gender ideals in socially structured specific practices, there are a variety of ways to do them. Specific forms of gender are available, encouraged, and permitted, and because the forms depend on one's position in these social relations, we must speak of masculini*ties* and feminini*ties*. Accordingly, gender must be viewed as *structured action*—what people do under specific social structural constraints (Messerschmidt 1993, 1997). The key to understanding the maintenance of existing gendered social structures is the accomplishment of gender through social interaction (West and Fenstermaker 1995). Social actors perpetuate and transform social structures within the same interaction; simultaneously, these structures constrain and enable gendered social action. The result is the ongoing social construction of gender relations. Structured action theory is specifically relevant to the study of teenage violence. As James Short (1997, 4) concludes after reviewing criminological literature on violent crime: "The linkage of . . . micro- and macrosocial levels of explanation is vital to the understanding and explanation of violent crime." That is, theory that connects social action (micro) with social structure (macro) is essential to the comprehension of adolescent male violence.

The Salience of Gender

The salience of gender relations to influencing crime varies by social situation. Although gender construction is ubiquitous, the significance of gender shifts from context to context: In one situation gender may be important to actuating crime; in another, class, race, or other social variables may be more important. In other words, gender is not absolute and is not always significant in every social setting in which crime is realized; that is, accountability to gender is not always, in every social situation, critical to the social construction of crime. Indeed, structured action theory is *not* a general theory of crime because masculinity (and femininity) varies in salience by social situation (Alder and Polk 1996; Messerschmidt 1997).

Nevertheless, social relations of gender—like class and race—variously join us in a common relationship to others—we share gendered structural space. Consequently, common or shared blocks of gendered knowledge and practices evolve through interaction in which particular gender ideals and activities differ in significance. Through such interaction, gender becomes institutionalized, permitting, for example, men and women to draw on such existing but previously formed ways of thinking and acting to construct particular gender identities for specific settings. The particular criteria of gender identities thus are embedded in the social situations and recurrent practices by which social relations are structured (Giddens 1989).

Gender, Power, and Difference

Power is an important structural feature of gender relations. But, in addition—and specifically with regard to masculinity (because this study concentrates on adolescent masculinities)—socially organized power relations among men are constructed historically on the bases of race, class, and sexual preference. In other words, in specific contexts some men (and some women) have greater power than other men (or other women); the capacity to exercise power is, for the most part, a reflection of one's position in social relationships. Consequently, heterosexual men and women exercise greater power than do gay men and lesbians; upper-class men and women exercise greater power than do working-class men and women; and white men and women wield greater power than do men and women of color. Power, then, is a relationship that structures social interaction not only between men and women but among men (and among women) as well. Nevertheless, power is not absolute and at times may actually shift in relation to different axes of power and powerlessness. That is, in one situation a working-class man may, for example, exercise power (e.g., as a patriarchal husband), whereas in another situation he may experience powerlessness (e.g., as a factory worker). Accordingly, masculinity and femininity can only be understood as fluid, relational, and situational constructs.

Hegemonic, Subordinated, and Oppositional Masculinities

Connell's (1987, 1995) notion of "hegemonic masculinity"—the culturally idealized form of masculinity in a given historical and social setting—is relevant here. Hegemonic masculinity varies over time, across societies, and among institutions in society. In any specific time and place—such as whole societies or institutions (e.g., schools and corporations)—hegemonic masculinity is culturally honored, glorified, and extolled at the symbolic level and through practice. Moreover, it is constructed in relation to "subordinated masculinities" (based on race, class, and sexual preference, for example), to "oppositional masculinities" (those that explicitly resist and possibly challenge hegemonic forms), and to femininities. In fact, hegemonic masculinity is the dominant form of masculinity in a given milieu in which other types of masculinities are subordinated or opposed—not eliminated. For example, in the secondary school social setting, we are likely to find representations of hegemonic masculinities (e.g., "cool guys" and "jocks"), subordinated masculinities (e.g., gay boys, "wimps," and "nerds"), and oppositional masculinities (e.g., "freaks" and "tough guys"). Ethnographies of secondary schooling in Britain, Australia, and the United States consistently report such masculine power relationships (see Connell 1996 for a review).

The relationship between specifically hegemonic and subordinated masculinities reveals a major social structural feature of gender relations—sexuality. Indeed, in industrialized societies heterosexuality is deemed normative, whereas "deviant" and subordinated sexualities are ridiculed, policed, and repressed. Not surprisingly, heterosexuality becomes a fundamental indication of hegemonic masculinity; gay (and "wimp" and "nerd") masculinities are subordinated to heterosexual masculinities; and sexuality merges with other social structures to help construct power relations among men.

Moreover, when hegemonic masculinity is refined further, we find that it emphasizes practices toward authority, control, independence, competitive individualism, aggressiveness, and the capacity for violence (Messerschmidt 1993). Concerning aggressiveness and capacity for violence, Sandra Walklate (1995, 97) argues that these aspects of hegemonic masculinity are extensive in industrialized societies—from the cultural conceptions of hero to the "cut and thrust" of political debate. "While one may value physical prowess, and the other verbal prowess, the need to 'win' over one's opponent constitutes a thread of continuity between the two." Anne Campbell (1993, 30–31) agrees, arguing that the connection between masculinity and violence is emphasized throughout the culture:

> It is men, not women, who slay dragons and fight in defense of the inno-
> cent. The literary heroes of boys' worlds are fearless warriors, flying
> aces, crime fighters. From Tom and Jerry to the Teenage Mutant Ninja
> Turtles, from Superman to Indiana Jones, it is males who both use and
> receive violence. . . . And because it is so tightly tied to masculinity, ag-
> gression becomes central to the notion of manhood.

Indeed, the cultural connection between hegemonic masculinity and violence normalizes and legitimizes "men's access to violence as a personal
and political resource" (Walklate 1995, 98).

Hegemonic masculinity, then, as the culturally and situationally dominant discourse and practice, influences but does not determine masculine
behavior. Hegemonic masculinity underpins the conventions applied in
the enactment and reproduction of masculinities—the lived patterns of
meanings, which as they are experienced as practice, appear as recipro-
cally confirming. As such, hegemonic masculinity shapes a sense of reality for most men and is continually renewed, recreated, defended, and
modified through practice. And yet it is at times resisted, limited, altered,
and challenged. As Barrie Thorne (1993, 106) notes, "Individuals and
groups develop varied forms of accommodation, reinterpretation, and re-
sistance to ideologically hegemonic patterns." Consequently, hegemonic
masculinity operates as "on-hand" to be actualized into practice in a
range of different circumstances. It provides a conceptual framework that
is materialized in the design of social structures and, therefore, materialized in daily practices and interactions.

At times and under certain social conditions men construct "oppositional masculinities" that in one way or another are extrinsic to and represent significant breaks from hegemonic masculinity, and may actually
threaten its dominance. For example, such various oppositional masculine practices as rejection of work in the paid labor market and rebellion
against "authority" in secondary schools are constructed from specific social settings. Hegemonic masculine practice is not merely adaptive and

incorporative; authentic transgressions within and beyond it occur under specific social conditions.

The concepts "hegemonic," "subordinated," and "oppositional" masculinities permit investigation of the different ways men experience their everyday worlds from their particular positions in society and how they relate to other men and women. Although most men attempt to express some aspects of hegemonic masculinity through speech, dress, physical appearance, activities, and relationships with others, these social signs of masculinity are associated with the specific context of individual action and are self-regulated within that context. Consequently, aspects of various masculinities can exist simultaneously. For example, a boy who rebels against "authority" in school (oppositional) may also engage in dominating and controlling practices of girls (hegemonic). Thus masculinity is based on a social construct that reflects unique circumstances and relationships—a social construction that is renegotiated in each particular context. In other words, social actors self-regulate their behavior and make specific choices in specific contexts. In this way, then, men construct varieties of masculinities through specific practices. And by emphasizing diversity in masculine construction, we achieve a more fluid and situated approach to our understanding of masculinity and crime.

Doing Masculinity and Violence

When men enter a social setting, they undertake practices which demonstrate that they are "manly." Aspects of social settings, social occasions, and social activities provide resources for doing masculinity (West and Zimmerman 1987). *Masculine resources* are contextually available practices (e.g., bullying, fighting, engaging in sexuality, and acting like a "gentleman") that can be drawn upon so that men and boys can demonstrate to others they are "manly." Resources appropriate for masculine construction change situationally. Thus men use the resources at their disposal to communicate masculinity to others. Because of its connection to hegemonic masculinity, for many men violence serves as a suitable resource for constructing masculinity. That is, individuals who occasionally turn to violence as a masculine resource have come to accept the hegemonic masculine notion of aggressiveness and capacity for violence. This acceptance of violence as a means of doing masculinity effectively predisposes such individuals toward violence, providing a resource for affirming a particular type of masculinity. Thus the term "predisposition" is used here *not* as a stable trait developed early in life and continuing throughout the life course relatively unchanged. Rather, predisposition refers to the appropriation of a particular masculine resource in a specific milieu that constructs a tendency or an inclination to act in distinct ways during certain forms of social interaction.

Masculinity Challenges

The significance of masculine accomplishment (as pointed out earlier) is socially situated and thus is intermittent. That is, certain occasions present themselves as more effectively intimidating for demonstrating and affirming masculinity. As Coleman (1990, 196) states, "Such an occasion is where a man's 'masculinity' risks being called into question." Because the taken-for-granted masculinity of a man or boy can be challenged in certain contexts, sex category is particularly salient; it is, as David Morgan (1992, 47) put it, "more or less explicitly put on the line" and doing masculinity can generate a distinct type of masculinity. Such *masculinity challenges* are contextual interactions that result in masculine degradation. Masculinity challenges arise from interactional threats and insults from peers, teachers, parents, and from situationally defined masculine expectations that are not achievable. Both, in various ways, proclaim a man or boy subordinate in contextually defined masculine terms. Because doing masculinity is an ongoing concern (West and Fenstermaker 1995), masculinity challenges may *motivate* social action toward masculine resources (e.g., bullying and/or fighting) that correct the subordinating social situation, and various forms of crime can be the result (Messerschmidt 1993, 1997). Given that such interactions question, undermine, and/or threaten one's masculinity, only contextually "appropriate" masculine practices can help overcome the challenge.

Social action is never simply an autonomous event but is amalgamated into larger assemblages—what Swidler (1986, 273) calls "strategies of action" or "persistent ways of ordering action through time." The cultural ideals of hegemonic masculinity encourage specific lines of gendered action, and social structures shape the capacities from which gendered strategies of action are constructed over time. Men and boys apply the ideals of hegemonic masculinity to the situations that face them in everyday life, and in the process pursue a gendered strategy of action (Hochschild 1989). From this perspective, then, social action is often designed with an eye to one's gender accountability, both individually and situationally. Individuals who have accepted hegemonic masculine notions of aggressiveness and capacity for violence as a masculine resource may apply such notions to situational events that involve masculinity challenges; such individuals are predisposed to violence in particular milieus, such as schools. The result is that differing types of violence by men and boys, depending upon the social setting, can be a form of social practice invoked for accomplishing masculinity under threatening social conditions.

Not all predisposed individuals are motivated toward violence, especially if they do not experience masculinity challenges. Similarly, those predisposed individuals who do experience masculinity challenges may nevertheless not engage in violence; that is, the situational *opportunities* may disallow the possibility of violence as a resource for responding to the masculinity challenge. For example, an opportunity for sexual and assaultive violence requires access to an "appropriate" victim; if such a victim is unavailable, violence does not result.

This study examines the construction and formation of masculinities through violent social action. Structured action theory is used to explore the ways masculinities are constructed through interaction within the particular social context of home, school, and adolescence. In short, to understand male working-class adolescent violence/nonviolence, we must appreciate how structure and action are woven inextricably into the ongoing activities of violent predisposition, masculinity challenges, motivation, opportunity, and the resulting violent or nonviolent masculinities.

A Theorized Life History

This study investigates adolescent male perpetrators of sexual and assaultive violence in the context of their entire lives, from their earliest memories to the point at which I encountered them. Such life history accounts lead to an understanding of the stages and critical periods in the processes of violent and nonviolent masculine development and to an understanding of how the particular individual is both enabled and constrained by structural position. Criminology reports very little about the life histories of violent adolescent offenders and especially little about their comparisons to nonviolent boys. Although some recent criminological work contributes notably to our understanding of adolescent masculinities and crime (Collison 1996; Hagedorn 1998), no life history research on adolescent masculinity and violence exists and no studies on youth violence explore why any given adolescent male engages in one type of violence over another. Additionally, criminology historically has been haunted by (but has never addressed adequately) the question of why boys who grow up simultaneously in the same or similar social milieus progress in different directions throughout the course of their lives. Finally, feminist studies of sex offenders ignore adolescent males who sexually assault younger children. Feminist studies that focus on rapists' accounts of their sexual violence have used exclusively adult male samples, failing to explore how life history affects eventual engagement with sexual violence (Beneke 1982; Levine and Koenig 1983; Scully 1990).

The primary goal of this study is to glean considerable and telling information from a modest sample of white working-class boys who engaged in different forms of violence and to compare these violent boys to a small group of white working-class boys who avoided involvement in any type of violence. By scrutinizing each detailed life history, we shall begin to learn the social processes involved in becoming violent or nonviolent. I believe the study has several significant strengths. First, the boys I interviewed reflect the serious (dark) end of the delinquent behavior continuum and represent two types of offender about whom criminologists must genuinely be concerned—sexual and assaultive adolescent males. Here *sexual offenders* are boys from fifteen to eighteen years of age who, by coercion or manipulation, engaged in sexual contact (e.g., fondling and/or penetration) with individuals legally unable to give informed consent. All the boys I interviewed were *exclusively* sex offenders; that is, they denied engaging in any other type of crime and had no official record of committing any other type of crime. The *assaultive offenders* I interviewed are boys from fifteen to eighteen years of age who acted in a nonsexual physically violent way against at least one other person—there exist no official records of them committing a sexually violent act and they all denied engaging in any sexual offense—although they may have committed such other nonviolent crimes as property and drug offenses. Thus, in terms of violence, these boys are *exclusively* assaultive offenders. The *nonviolent boys* I studied are fifteen to eighteen years of age who had not admitted committing, nor been formally charged with committing, a violent act, or admitted engaging in violence (but never formally charged) for a brief period early in their lives (and at a young age) and thereafter adopted an exclusively nonviolent pattern of behavior. In structuring these three categories, then, I studied boys who engaged in two different types of violence and their peers who were exclusively nonviolent.

Second, demographically matched comparison groups are included to help explore the reasons for sexual and assaultive offending as well as the reasons for nonviolence. Boys were matched according to the following demographic characteristics:

Boys in all three categories:
- sex (male)
- age (15–18)
- social class (working class)
- race (white)

Sex offenders:
- contact sexual violence (fondling to penetration)
- age of at least one victim (14 or younger)
- sex of victim (male or female)
- victim relationship (relative or acquaintance)

Assaultive offenders:
- contact physical violence (assault)
- age of victim (14–50)
- sex of victim (male or female)
- victim relationship (stranger, relative, or acquaintance)

Finally, the life history method is particularly relevant because it richly documents personal experiences and transformations over time. A life history records "the relation between the social conditions that determine practice and the future social world that practice brings into being" (Connell 1995, 89). The life history method is what Thomas and Znaniecki (1927) characterized as the "perfect" type of sociological material. Such classics of criminology as Clifford Shaw's (1930) *The Jack Roller* and Edwin Sutherland's (1937) *The Professional Thief* illustrate "the power of life-history data to illuminate the complex processes of criminal offending" (Sampson and Laub 1993, 203). Indeed, the life history method is experiencing a resurgence in the social sciences, including the sociology of masculinities (Connell 1995; Messner 1992), the sociology of sexualities (Dowsett 1996), and the sociology of crime (Finkelhor and Yllo 1985; Miller 1986; Sampson and Laub 1993; Goetting 1999). The revival is due in part to the fact that life histories tap continuous "lived experiences" of individuals. That is, the method demands a close evaluation of the meaning of social life for those who enact it, revealing *their* experiences, practices, and social world. As Robert Agnew (1990, 271) points out, the accounts of those involved in crime "may be the only way of obtaining accurate information on the individual's internal states and those aspects of the external situation that the individual is attending to."

In addition to in-depth documentation of an individual's conceptual world and the representations of such conceptions through practice, the life history links the social and historical context in which both are embedded. As Connell (1995, 89) points out, "The project that is documented in a life-history story is itself the relation between the social conditions that determine practice and the future social world that practice brings into being. That is to say, life-history method always concerns the making of social life through time. It is literally history."

Thus one salient feature of the life history method in exploring sexual and/or assaultive violence by boys is that it permits an in-depth understanding of the "interplay between structural fact and personal experience" (Connell 1991, 143). The life history can reveal what other methods can hide or obscure. The research here embraces a *theorized life history* as the specific method because the interviewing and interpretation are based on structured action theory (Connell 1991; Dowsett 1996). This particular procedure is "not a process of theorization by generalization, but a systematic method of investigating the operation of social processes through the recounted experiences of individual lives" (Dowsett 1996, 50).

Sample

Life history research does not target large and representative samples from which to draw bold generalizations. Rather, its goal is to uncover patterns and to provide useful cases that signal contributing factors to violence and nonviolence by white working-class adolescent males. Indeed, the sampling procedure can be best described as "stratified purposeful sampling" (Patton 1990, 172–174) to fit the theorized life history method.

First, ten white working-class adolescent males currently incarcerated or undergoing private counseling for sexual or assaultive violence were selected to match the demographic variables identified earlier (variables that match the features of wider samples) and then were categorized according to offense type: "sex offender" (five boys) or "assaultive offender" (five boys). I chose incarcerated boys and those voluntarily in private counseling to avoid limiting the sample to boys officially processed in the juvenile justice system. The incarcerated boys were identified by prison personnel who obtained the informed consent of the boys *and* their parents or guardians before I interviewed them. The boys in private counseling were similarly identified by therapists prior to informed-consent interviews.

Second, five white working-class adolescent males who denied committing, and had not been formally charged with committing, a sexually violent and/or assaultive offense (or admitted committing an assaultive act in the past but for a very short period of time) were selected (according to relevant demographic variables) with the assistance of representatives from the Boys and Girls Club and the use of a "snowballing" approach and were categorized as "nonviolent boys."

Finally, for each group—sex offenders, assaultive offenders, and nonviolent boys—I obtained a "mix" of boys from different family configurations (e.g., adoptive parents versus biological parents; violent versus nonviolent households) as well as rural and urban areas. This "maximum-variation" sampling procedure provided a selection of boys from a wide range of home life and other background situations. I interviewed three boys—one representing each of the three categories—who simultaneously grew up in the same milieu (lived in the same neighborhood and attended the same school). The race and social class of the entire sample remained constant (white working class). All the boys in this study began from relatively similar starting points—gender and race privilege coupled with class disadvantage.[4]

Some argue that we learn little from such a small sample. However, a detailed investigation of a few case studies often illuminates contributing factors concealed by other methodologies. Dowsett (1996) points out that in other disciplines, such as the medical community, scholars frequently publish research based on a limited number of clinically observed cases. For example, a 1990 article published in the *American Journal of Public Health* documented (p. 44):

> HIV seroconversions in gay men, related, it seems, exclusively to receptive oral intercourse with swallowed ejaculate. Given the ongoing unresolved debate about the likelihood of HIV transmission through oral-genital sex, this was a sensational finding. The article, however, was based on two cases, and although the authors' conclusions were properly cautionary, the example demonstrates that the chief concern need not always be the sampling method and sample size.

Nevertheless, nine case studies are not a representative sample and, therefore, my conclusions are only suggestive.[5] However, as with the article just cited, the life stories reported in Chapters 2, 3, and 5 simultaneously show that important aspects of sexual and assaultive violence by white working-class teenage males have been overlooked but are an extremely rich source for further investigation and theory building. As Solomin Kobrin (1982, 153) pointed out, life histories reveal the more "elusive elements of deviant behavior that are often difficult to capture in quantifiable variables." Each life story deepens and augments our understanding of the situational accomplishment of masculinities and of the eventual use of violence or nonviolence as a result of personal life history.

Data Collection

The theorized life history method implemented here involved voluntary and confidential one-on-one tape-recorded "informal conversational interviews" (Patton 1990, 280–282). These conversations were conducted in private, secluded rooms and were completed in two meetings of three hours each. The conversations were fluid, allowing each boy to take the lead rather than merely respond to topical questions. The goal was to grasp each boy's unique viewpoint—his personal vision of the world. This interview method involves the interviewer judiciously engaging the boy, "working interactionally to establish the discursive bases from which the respondent can articulate his or her relevant experiences" (Holstein and Gubrium 1995, 47).

This does not mean, however, that the conversations were unstructured. On the contrary, each conversation attempted to reflect the situational accomplishment of masculinities and the eventual use of violence or nonviolence as a result of personal life history. As such, the interviews drew on the insights of structured action theory. I specifically sought detailed descriptions of practices (what a boy did, not solely how he felt) and accounts of interaction in families, peer/leisure groups, and schools. The conversations touched on intimate and sensitive areas of personal life and relationships. Topical examples I explored include (1) the division of labor between men and women in the boy's household and in the peer/leisure groups of which he is a member; (2) the power dynamics between male and female adults, between adults and children, among boys, and between boys and girls at school and in peer groups; (3) any masculine mentoring during childhood and adolescence; (4) his sexual awakening, how he managed it, and how images of sexuality were conveyed to him; (5) the meaning and practices of masculinity and violence through-out his life course and how both were represented to him; (6) the tensions and predispositions in these processes and the way they changed over time; and (7) all masculinity challenges and violent events over each boy's life course.

Limitations of the Study

Although life history research provides rich areas of criminological re-search, it is not without limitation. Indeed, there are traditional problems related to investigator effects; for example, the investigator recounts "only part of the story" (Short 1982, 135). However, as James Short (p. 135) re-sponds, this criticism should not be seen as unique to life history data: "Dif-ferent methods tell different parts of a story and tell them differently." As we know, all knowledge is partial and situated, derived in part from the re-searcher's authority and privilege (Richardson 1990). Life stories must be seen as active constructs in themselves, jointly developed by interviewer and interviewee. In critically assessing my place and position during each conversation, I followed suggestions of feminist sociologists that interview-ers attempt to give up *"authority* over the people we study, but not the re-sponsibility of *authorship* of our texts" (Reinhartz, 1992, p. 28). This in-volved developing strategies to empower boys during our interaction. For example, I met each boy twice, using the second conversation to carefully review together the content of the earlier conversation. This helped break down hierarchy, encourage boys to find and speak the "correctness" of their stories, and avoid treating each boy as simply an object of study.

In addition, the possibilities that respondents may, for example, lack memory of key events and/or issues or simply attempt to deceive the in-terviewer is always an issue in such methodology. However, I agree with Robert Agnew (1990), who argues that there is no a priori reason to as-sume that boys are more likely to be dishonest or subject to faulty mem-ory during, for example, life history interviews than they are when partic-ipating in such other procedures as self-report questionnaires and large-scale surveys. In each of these three methods, answers to questions reflect the "respondents' perception of reality and events" (p. 269). Given that such "contaminants" may occur in any social science methodology, I chose to study what is expressed in each conversation and to treat each life history as a *situational truth.* As Ann Goetting (1999, 20) points out, life stories are not simply "true" representations of an objective "reality"; rather, the interpretations of both interviewer and interviewee "combine to create a particular view of reality."

Of necessity, I have built in research strategies that increase the credibility of findings. Prior to commencing an interview in a secluded room, I explained that risk of identification was negligible inasmuch as all interview information would be identified by a number only, stored in a secure facility, and destroyed by me at the conclusion of the study. Moreover, I pointed out that interview conversations would be treated with strict confidence and never made available to another person or agency and that certain identifying details would be changed. Further, I obtained informed consent prior to the interview. I also indicated that the final results of the research would be published in a manner that fully protected his anonymity, his family members, and all others mentioned during the interview. Also, I addressed topics in different ways and at varying times during the interview. Interestingly, the answers rarely varied.

Finally, in addition to joint construct, boys' accounts, like all interview data, probably are affected by meanings that are external to the conversation—such as what boys learned in treatment and/or incarceration. Therefore, I specifically discussed with each boy whether his responses were shaped by such experiences; that is, was his past behavior reinterpreted during our conversations in light of his experiences in treatment or incarceration. I consistently asked each boy to recapture the past and respond as to how he conceptualized events at the time of enactment. In all cases, boys were able to distinguish what they learned in treatment and/or incarceration about their behavior from what they felt at the particular time in the past. Moreover, I discussed with therapists and counselors the nature of any treatment received by each boy. For all participants in this study, gender and masculinity were never a remedial part of their rehabilitation.

Although it is important to verify factual information and consistency in storytelling, the primary task of the life history researcher is not to establish an alleged "truth" but to describe—as stated earlier—how each particular life story assembles a specific situational truth. What is critical is that the life story is "true" for the interviewee at that moment—that it captures the boy's subjective reality and his unique definition of the situation. The aim is not simply to relate a particular life history to other cases in the project and to previous research findings (which I do) but also to grasp each case for what it tells us about that specific case. In short, each conversation attempted to comprehend the life course, formation of masculinities, and use of violence or nonviolence as outcomes of a personal trajectory constrained by one's social structural position.

Data Analysis

Data analysis had two stages. First, tape-recorded conversations were transcribed and thoroughly analyzed, and individual case studies were prepared (Chapters 2, 3, and 5). Second, the life histories within the three designated groups (sex offenders, assaultive offenders, and nonviolent boys) were dissected to define similarities and differences among the pathways to differing forms of violence (Chapter 4) and nonviolence (Chapter 6). Consistent with other theorized life history methodology, the intent here is not simply to present biography but to explain social process through the life history data (Connell 1995; Dowsett 1996).

The chapters that follow capture each boy's experience in *his* words. As such, we "see" how individual social action and interaction with others are embedded in social structural constraints. Moreover, by comparing individual life stories we can establish links among boys whose lives are quite different but who are affected by similar race and class position. In other words, we can discover the interconnections among boys who live in a shared social context. Accordingly, theorized life history methodology helps to register patterns in lives that other methodologies render invisible. The consistencies in the life story accounts demonstrate there is, in fact, a world of shared masculine meanings that boys express differently in the course of their lives. And, as shown throughout this book, there is much here to offer in our attempt to understand youth violence generally and the school shootings in particular.

Finally, a brief note on the title of the book, *Nine Lives*. I chose it for two reasons. First, and most obvious, the book is about the lives of nine boys. Second, as revealed in the life stories, each boy in his own unique way "bounces back"—like a cat with nine lives—from what he sees as a degrading masculine social situation and reconstructs his masculinity in specific ways.

NOTES

1. An exception is the important work of Doug Pryor (1996). Unfortunately, this book examines only *adult* males who sexually abused children.

2. Anne-Marie Ambert (1995, 182) coined the term "peer abuse" to refer to "acts, omissions, as well as words that *intentionally* inflict physical, and/or psychological, and/or social injury to a peer or peers from an age-mate or from a group of age-mates." I use Ambert's definition in this book.

3. Although race and class are equally important to gender, this study specifically concentrates on masculinity. Initially I planned to study all three relations but found it incredibly difficult during the interviews to address simultaneously issues concerning race, class, and masculinity. I would still be interviewing if I had chosen to examine all three!

4. I follow John Hagan's (1992, 12) suggestion that we structure research so as to learn more about the way in which class relates to crime throughout the life course. In this study, all three categories are *working-class* boys (based on the economic position of their parent[s] or legal guardian[s]), yet boys who take different paths throughout their life course. Here "social class" is defined as "a group of people who share the same position in the production system" and "working class" refers to those who work for a wage and do not control any portion of the means of production (Beirne and Messerschmidt 1995, 60, 64).

5. Following the suggested procedure of Glassner and Loughlin (1987, 21–22), I report as evidence in Chapters 2, 3, and 5 only those interviews in which boys are consistent in their stories throughout the conversations. I rejected one interview because of continual inconsistencies (I learned later this interviewee was severely medicated) and another interview because the offender was unable to discuss further his past relationship with his father (he broke down crying). The remaining four interviews (of a total sample of fifteen) are not reported in this book because of what is referred in the literature as a "saturation-of-information" effect (Seidman 1998, 48). In all three categories I reached a point where I began to hear very similar types of information being reported—I was no longer hearing anything new. Therefore, these four stories are not part of the discussion because they added nothing new to the data and would have produced only repetition. Moreover, I do not discuss how the boys were caught nor the resolution of their cases as this information may reveal their identity. Finally, my selection of white, working-class boys limits any generalization to racial minority working-class boys as well as middle-class boys. Clearly, there is a need for life history research on these latter two categories of boys.

2

Sam, John, and Zack

In this chapter I present the life stories of Sam (age 18), John (age 18), and Zack (age 15). All three boys, at certain points in their lives, undertook paths that involved sexual coercion and/or manipulation of children. The boys sexually victimized females they knew personally and all three displayed serious problems interacting with peers. Sam grew up in a nonviolent home, whereas John and Zack experienced severe physical, sexual, and verbal abuse at home. These three case studies are uniquely juxtaposed, allowing the opportunity to investigate the similarities and differences between a boy raised in a nonviolent home who became a sex offender and two boys reared in violent families who also became sex offenders. The chapter advances literature on sexual violence through its comparison of boys from different family configurations and its concentration on changing masculinities in the life histories of adolescent sex offenders. We begin with Sam.

Sam

Sam was a boyish-looking eighteen-year-old who was markedly animated while articulating his life story. He was so excited about telling me his story that he came to the interviews with detailed lists of important episodes and circumstances in his life. He also pointed out at several stages of our conversations that the interviews helped him understand the past and that he hoped his story would help others.

Sam was from a working-class suburb where he lived with his two adoptive parents and younger biological sister. Like other members of the "respectable" working class, the family owned its own home when Sam was growing up. Sam became a member of this family when he and his sister were abandoned by their biological mother.

Sam and his sister were assigned to a variety of foster homes, eventually being adopted when Sam was five by his current foster parents. When Sam was younger, his "mom" and "dad" (what he calls them) worked at a service industry job and a skilled manual job, respectively, generating a modest working-class income. Sam's mother did all the cooking at home, as well as the shopping for food and other necessities. The kids helped their mother with daily household cleaning. Their father, according to Sam, "mowed the lawn, loafed around, and worked with his tools."

Sam thus grew up among explicit practices defining "men's work" and "women's work" at home and in the workplace. Further, these practices nourished Sam's idea of future labor force participation: Sam wanted to "work with tools" after finishing high school. Indeed, by the time he was in high school Sam had his own automobile that was just as "decked out as Dad's."

Sam reported substantial family cohesiveness and stability, describing very close contact with both parents: "We went on many vacations together as a family—going camping, fishing, and hunting. We had a great time together." Sam indicated that he experienced an especially warm and affectionate family relationship (discipline was verbal, not physical) and remembered specifically bonding with his father: "He taught me all about tools and everything else, and I used to be able to hand him the tools when he was working on trailer trucks." Moreover, Sam's father had the power in the home: "Dad was the one who kept in control over everything." Sam's mother and the kids always yielded to his dad's decisions: "We always looked to Dad; he was the one who took control."

Sam obviously identified with his father, who was his initial model for developing a specific type of maleness. Indeed, when I asked Sam if he was concerned about having approval from his father, he stated, "Yeah, that meant a lot to me, Dad telling me I did a good job helping him." Sam's interviews clearly showed that within the family a substantial commitment toward, and a smooth reproduction of, a masculinity was constructed by Sam that included numerous practices such as working with tools, fishing and hunting, male power in the household, and manual labor. And Sam expanded his conception of masculinity at the time: "Success at work, power, money, strong, being like Dad."

At school Sam collided with an unsettling social situation. In elementary school, after breaking away from a group of "troublemakers," Sam was subjected to consistent peer abuse because of his physical size and shape (he was shorter and heavier than the other boys), eventually to the extent of "living in fear of going to school." Sam did not do well in school because, according to him, he worried more about being verbally abused than doing schoolwork and was placed in special education courses. During his eighth-grade year his classmates were recalled as making the following remark: "Everybody looked at me like 'Oh, there is something wrong with him.'"

Being verbally abused about shortness and obesity and feeling rejection for being "slow" intellectually extended through eighth grade and into high school. Although Sam observed numerous instances of boys fighting at school because of peer abuse, he did not respond directly to the abusing classmates because of his physical size—he did not want to be "beat up." As a result, Sam constantly watched his back, watched where he was stepping, "always really nervous at school, because people picked on me." When asked if he discussed the peer abuse with his parents, Sam replied:

> Yeah, I talked to my dad about it. My dad kept telling me to fight back, let them know I was a tough guy. He would tell me: "Hit them right back. Don't let them get to you, don't let them bug you." And I wanted to fight back but I didn't feel like I was strong, like I could fight back like dad said.

Thus Sam experienced embarrassment in school for poor grades and for being a "special ed kid." He had feelings of masculine inadequacy because of his physical size and shape, as well as a sense of powerlessness for his inability to fight back as his father recommended and as his peers expected. Consequently, Sam became a loner at school and stopped discussing the abuse with his father because he did not want to disappoint him. As he states:

> They would call me "porky," a "wimp," that I couldn't stick up for myself, that I was a "mama's boy." I wasn't worth anything according to them. I felt like I was a girl, someone they [the popular boys] shouldn't hang around or talk to. So, of course I didn't tell Dad, and my loner lifestyle.

The boys who abused Sam were "the popular ones," boys who played sports, attended parties, and had lots of friends. When I asked Sam how they identified him as a "wimp," he replied that they would try to get me to fight with them. They would say, "Come on fat boy, fight." But they were all tall and strong so I'd run away. I wouldn't stay around them. And they'd call me names.

Sam wanted to fight back like other kids and as his father had taught him but felt he was not strong enough. Consequently, Sam did not have any friends at school: "I wasn't like one of them; I wasn't one that had friends to hang out with."

Sam clearly was questioning his ability to protect himself from the ongoing "degradation ceremonies" at school, unable to control such a threatening environment. In fact, he was incapable of making the appropriate masculine response—fighting back physically—which he had learned through interaction at school and from his special mentor (father). And significantly, he could *not* discuss this situation with his parents because he felt he would "let them down" for not being able to handle the situation as his father instructed. Thus by the time he was fifteen years old Sam lacked masculine resources and therefore felt extremely powerless, distressed, and subordinate at school.

During his freshman year in high school Sam developed a sexual consciousness in which he sexually objectified and desired women. He learned this from interaction at school and not from his parents. As Sam states: "Kids were talking at school about 'blow jobs,' 'getting laid,' telling dirty jokes, and about having sex and stuff like that." Sam constantly heard the popular boys' "sex talk" about sexual objectification of girls as well as heterosexual exploits and experiences. He desired to participate but, because he was a "virgin" and a loner, could not share the "sex-talk" comaraderie. It was schoolboy chat, then, that was Sam's source of information about sexuality. So it was during his freshman year that Sam became very interested in heterosexuality: he wanted to experience it and "learn what it was like." Clearly, this development had its gender component. When asked why he wanted to experience sex, Sam added,

> I thought, well, I'm a guy, so this is something that every guy does, that I want to be part of this. I want to be like the other guys. I want to know what it feels like, I want to know what goes on.

Sam knew several girls at school with whom he wished to have a sexual relationship, but because of the constant peer abuse "I didn't think I was good enough. I didn't have the trust enough to gain access to a girl. I didn't think any girl would be interested in me." Thus Sam clearly objectified and sought out girls in order to be "like the other guys" but was unable to fulfill this situationally defined masculine criterion.

By age fifteen, then, Sam was experiencing degradation ceremonies at school about his physical size and shape, as well as earning poor grades. His inability to "fight back" severely haunted him and significantly added to his lack of masculine resources and accompanying negative masculine self-esteem. This masculine insecurity was further enhanced by his inability to be a "real man" through developing sexual relationships with girls his age.

Accordingly, Sam attempted to overcome his lack of masculine resources and thereby diminish the negative masculine feelings and situations through controlling and dominating behaviors involving the use of sexual power. Unable to be masculine by responding in a physically aggressive way to the people threatening him (i.e., the "popular guys") and incapable of developing sexual relationships with girls his age, Sam turned to the masculine behaviors that were available to him—expressing control and power over younger girls through sexuality.

During his freshman year Sam began babysitting a few neighbor girls (6–8 years old) in his house after school and then all day during the summer. It was Sam's idea to babysit and his parents instantly accepted, believing it was a splendid decision on Sam's part. During this year in high school—a time when he experienced most of the distressing events discussed earlier and when he "discovered" heterosexuality—Sam began to sexually assault some of the girls he babysat:

> I wanted to have some kind of sexual experience. And that didn't happen at school. I mean, I wasn't around other people, I didn't experience relationships with people my own age. And I started seeing the girls I babysat as being innocent and being able to take advantage of easily. I looked at how my life was, how I feared the people at school, so I figured I could get a girl I was babysitting easier. That's why I wanted to babysit.

The adults trusted Sam with the girls because in front of them he was gentle and caring toward them. The girls liked Sam, and he gained their trust. Indeed, becoming a babysitter was a major turning point in Sam's life. As he interprets it: "Babysitting gave me a place where I was in control because I was taking care of kids and I had control over them." When asked how he chose specific girls to abuse, Sam explained that he noticed some of the girls were "more quiet" and more vulnerable and therefore more easily exploitable.

Sam sexually assaulted (fondling and oral sex) two girls over a two-year period using manipulation strategies to gain access to them: "I kept gaining ways to manipulate, ways to like bribe, like act like I was helping them, act like I was doing good things for them, like playing games with them. For example, 'I'll play Nintendo with you if you do this for me.'" Sam stated that he did not blatantly physically threaten the girls he sexually assaulted. However, he would "wrestle with them and throw them around, and pretend that I know all this self-defense stuff, making it look like I was invincible, like I was strong, tough, and couldn't be hurt. That they couldn't fight back. Through that, that's what I used to scare them."

The following extended dialogue reveals what the sexual violence accomplished for Sam:

Q. How did it make you feel when you were able to manipulate the girls you were babysitting?

A. I was getting away with something that nobody else that I saw was getting away with. I felt that I was number one. I felt like I was better, like I was a better person, because I could play this little game with them and they didn't see what was going on. Like, I could trap 'em. It was like then they really didn't have much of a choice but to go along with what I wanted them to do.

Q. You felt special?

A. Yeah, because it was like I could manipulate anybody, because it was like I could put on a facade like as if I was a good person all the time. I would be such a nice person. I went to church, I did things for people, I acted nice. I would paint the image like I was a good boy. And all the while I was having sex with these girls.

Q. How did it make you feel when you sexually assaulted these two girls?

A. I didn't feel like I was small anymore, because in my own grade, my own school, with people my own age, I felt like I was a wimp, the person that wasn't worth anything. But when I did this to the girls, I felt like I was big, I was in control of everything.

Q. And you continued to sexually assault these girls?

A. Yes, that's why I kept doing it, 'cause I felt that control and I wanted that control more and more and more. And that's why it was hard for me to stop, because I'd have to return to that old me of being small and not being anything. I wasn't good at sports, and tough and strong and stuff, so I wasn't fitting in with anybody that was really popular. I was like a small person, someone that nobody really paid attention to. I was the doormat at school. People walked all over me and I couldn't fight back.

Q. *Did you feel you were entitled to these girls?*

A. I felt like I should be able to have sexual contact with anybody that I wanted to. And I couldn't do that with girls my own age. So I felt like, okay, I'll get it from the girls I was babysitting.

Q. *Why did you feel entitled to sex?*

A. Like, well, I'm a guy. I'm supposed to have sex. I'm supposed to be like every other guy. And so I'm like them, but I'm even better than them [popular boys], because I can manipulate. They don't get the power and the excitement. They have a sexual relationship with a girl. She can say what she wants and she has the choice. But the girls I babysat didn't have the choice. It was like I made it look like they had a choice, but when they stated their choice, if they said no, I like bugged them and bugged them until they didn't say no.

Q. *How did that make you feel in relation to the other males at school?*

A. I was like better than every other guy, because there was no way I could get rejected. It was like, okay, they can have their relationships, I'm gonna do whatever I want. I'm better than they are.

The control, power, and sexual arousal associated with the sexual domination of girls provided Sam with a contextually based masculine resource when other masculine resources were unavailable. Moreover, he was not simply adequate as a male but was now supermasculine. However, the sense of maleness derived from this violent practice had a short duration, lasting usually until he went back to school. Because the sexually violent behavior did not resolve the threatening masculine situation, Sam was faced with masculine self-doubts again and again. Thus his constant achievement of masculinity through continuous sexual assault of selected girls while babysitting them.

John

When I first met John, he looked sad, physically tattered, and tired. He was glancing around the room constantly—there was a bona fide paranoia about his demeanor. He quickly became trusting of me and candidly expressed a deep desire to detail his life story. After hearing what he had experienced in his life, I understood his subdued behavior during our initial conversation.

Like Sam, John grew up in a working-class environment. He, his younger brother (by one year), mother, and stepfather lived together on a farm. John and his brother were responsible for the outside chores (e.g., feeding the chickens) as well as some inside duties such as keeping their room clean. The stepfather worked at a skilled manual-labor job during the week and worked the farm on weekends. The boys' mother was unemployed outside the home but was responsible for shopping, cleaning, and cooking. However, John's mother rarely was home: "My mom was really inconsistent in my life. She walked in and out a lot. She was there sometimes and then sometimes not." And when his mother was around the house, there was not much contact between her and John: "She was there physically, but emotionally she wasn't there. She was just there to like feed me and give me shelter and then she'd be gone all over the place. She was drunk a lot." In fact, the only time his mother seemed to be around the house was at "dinner time" and to send the children "off to bed." Thus John spent the larger part of his early childhood and adolescence with his stepfather.

Like Sam, John grew up among conventional practices of "women's work" and "men's work." These practices similarly shaped John's perception of his future labor force participation: "I wanted to become a carpenter 'cause I liked building things. I really liked hands-on stuff, like building. I guess I learned that from my stepfather." John and his younger brother helped their stepfather work the farm, who was often critical of the boys' help. Yet he would occasionally praise John:

> I tried real hard to do good work. My stepfather always put me down, but he would sometimes tell me I did a good job helping him build stuff. That made me happy when he said that.

In short, John learned early in his life from his stepfather the importance of manual labor and its association with manhood.

Other than the work they did together, however, John had an extremely tortuous relationship with him. John's stepfather ignored him most of the time, and when he did interact with John it usually involved some type of verbal, physical, and/or sexual violence. Moreover, his stepfather was extremely violent toward John's mother, which most likely explains why she was around the house as little as possible: "I saw and heard my mom beat up and I experienced a lot of rape. I was beat on a lot, tormented. It was hell." I asked John to provide an example: "Well, when I was about six, my stepfather anally raped me and told me not to tell anyone. It was stuff like that. He was really violent." In addition to the sexual violence, there were physical beatings as well. John describes one occasion:

I remember one time me and my brother were screwing around with a bottle of shampoo. We were just little kids. We didn't know what it was, and we accidentally spilled some on the floor. And he got really pissed off about that, and he grabbed my brother and started hitting him. He whacked me on the side of the head and told us we were stupid, and he sent us to our room. While we were in our room we were talking, and he came in and put duct tape over our mouth.

John described many types of physical beatings in which he received a bloody nose, a split lip, and numerous bruises on his arms and legs. John suffered physical beatings about three times a week and was sexually assaulted by his stepfather about thirty times. John's mother never seemed to be around during the sexual and physical violence, and he never told her about it.

I never said anything. You know, when I was being fucked, my stepfather would tell me that he loved me but he also told me, "You know, you say anything and I'm gonna kill you." So I was confused and I'm not gonna open my mouth, because I don't want to die. So, you know, I just kept my mouth shut and did what I was told. I grew up thinking all this was normal.

The stepfather sexually abused John's brother as well, and once

he did it to both of us together. He had my brother anally rape me and me do the same to him, and he would do the same to us. And then after that he told us this is how you show affection but we better not tell anyone.

In addition, the stepfather frequently verbally abused John, calling him "a loser" and "a piece of shit." The stepfather was regularly drunk and would blame John for the violence by stating, "If you didn't piss me off I wouldn't have to do this" (physically beat him). As John states,

I began to walk on eggshells. I tried very hard not to make him angry. I tried very hard to stay away from him. But no matter what I did, it wasn't good enough for him. There was no pleasing him and I perceived myself as being worthless.

Thus during John's first fourteen years of life his stepfather was the only model of masculinity in his life (then his stepfather was arrested and convicted of the sexual violence). Indeed, in addition to such practices as working on the farm, carpentry, and other forms of manual labor, he learned from his stepfather that to be masculine a boy had to

be strong, there could be no flaws to me, that I had to set the example that if I am a man I have to be strong. I can't cry. I can't show people the soft side of me. And if that means beating somebody's face in, then that's what I had to do. I can't let anyone push me around, you know. I couldn't be this wimp. You gotta get them before they get you. I learned all that kinda stuff from him.

John's interaction with his stepfather clearly included an emphasis on male power, control over others, and the use of physical violence to solve interpersonal problems. Moreover, with his mother around infrequently, John's primary parental "affection" occurred during sexual victimization when his stepfather told John he "loved" him. There was little attentive supervision, John avoided the house as much as possible, and he frequently roamed the streets. In many ways, then, John grew up under working-class family conditions that were substantially different from Sam's.

School was not much better than home for John and reinforced the negative masculine self-esteem evolving at home. He was an average student in terms of schoolwork and attended school regularly from kindergarten through high school. However, when he was nine years old he began to experience agonizing peer abuse from other students: "In junior high, you know, people would put me down for the way I looked and for being small, and I didn't like being put down." John had good relations with his teachers but was quiet and reserved in the classroom. Asked why he acted this way in the classroom, John responded, "Because I didn't want to get laughed at if I said something stupid. So I didn't say nothing at all. I was basically a loner in school. I was by myself." Indeed, John did not have any friends his age at school or in his neighborhood "because nobody really liked me, because they just like pushed me away because I was small and they perceived that I wasn't worth anything. I didn't bother to go around kids my age." When in the company of peers, it seemed he was always abused: "They called me a 'klutz,' 'ugly,' 'weird looking,' 'wimp,' and they never picked me to play in games. And I couldn't fight back like other kids did." Asked why he did not respond to this abuse in a way other kids at school did and how his stepfather taught him, John stated, "I wanted to, but because I was small I would be killed."

John's unsettled masculine situation continued through eighth grade. He felt he had no friends and was unable to protect himself from his stepfather at home, from peers at school, and from kids in the neighborhood. Like Sam, John had no one with whom he could discuss the situation. Consequently, he felt alone, extremely powerless, and unfit to control his life. He was unable to respond adequately to such situations in the "appropriate" masculine way. He was incapable—as he observed other kids at school and his stepfather had instructed him—to put people in their place, fight back physically, and control and dominate others through violence if necessary. He felt helpless, he felt like a "wimp": "I believed what they said, that I was nothin', I was just a worthless wimp."

So by the time John was fourteen he, like Sam, attempted to overcome his lack of masculine resources and thereby diminish the negative masculine feelings and situations through controlling and dominating conduct involving the use of sexual power. Unwilling to respond to the abuse through physical violence, John turns to the only other masculine practice demonstrated at home: he sexually abused a seven-year-old neighbor boy.

Q. Tell me about this boy.

A. He was a neighbor that lived up the road. And I had built a tree fort. I used the tree fort to fuck him, 'cause no one could see and I was alone.

Q. Why this boy?

A. He liked me, he looked up to me, and he did anything I said.

Q. How did you get him alone in the tree fort?

A. I'd bribe him. I'd say, I'll give you this and that if you do this. I'd give him money, candy. I'd be nice to him. I'd play games with him. I'd be a friend to him.

Q. What about his parents?

A. They thought I was a really nice guy. I put out a really big image.

Q. Did you plan out the sexual assault of this neighbor boy?

A. Yeah, I had it all calculated. First I gained trust in his parents. I would take him bike riding and then I'd take him home if it was dark and say, "He's okay."

Q. So his parents trusted you?

A. I waited till I had their trust before I started to fuck him.

When John was being sexually victimized by his stepfather, he came to view the sexual violence as "normal sexuality." As John states, "I thought this was normal for a guy to do, especially a big man to a little one. And I said the same thing to the boy I fucked. It was sexually pleasing and I had power like my stepfather had over me. And I liked that power and control." During his eighth-grade year in school John sexually assaulted (anal and oral penetration) this boy four times in the tree fort.

Eventually John graduated from junior high and entered high school. High school was boring to John and seemed unimportant to his life plans. Because he wanted to be a carpenter, only courses that allowed him "to build things" were interesting. "Why am I learning about Aristotle?" he wondered and concluded that school was simply "an inconvenience" in his life. Moreover, the abuse that he received in junior high continued in high school: "I was pushed around a lot. I just happened to be the person who got in the way, and they just beat on me because of my looks and size and I couldn't fight back like other kids. In high school I kept to myself. I didn't talk to people." According to John, he did not "fit in" any "crowd" at school and was rejected by most kids. The popular athletic boys consistently chose him to degrade publicly: "The popular people—they was the bullies and I didn't like the bullies. I felt like a wimp because these guys used to put me down and say, 'You're a wimp, you can't do this and that.'" As in junior high, John did not fight back when bullied, primarily because of his physical size. As he put it:

I wanted to get back at them because my stepfather, when he would be beating on me he'd say, you know, you shouldn't cry, 'cause people are gonna think you're a wimp and beat on you more. And watching other kids get pushed around, and then they'd just turn around and belt the kid, and all these people watching would applaud them and say, "Yes, you got him." So I wanted to do that but couldn't so I just kind of walked out of the way. I wasn't a big, tough guy, like everyone expected me to be.

When asked if it bothered him that he could not respond to the abuse by fighting back, John stated,

Yeah, it made me feel like a wimp that I could not fight. I wish I could have been tall, because all these people are six feet something, and I'm just this little five-foot kid. So, I kind of felt out of place.

Moreover, until high school John's primary knowledge and experience of sexuality consisted of being the *victim* of his stepfather's violence and the *victimizer* of the neighbor boy. John conceptualized this as "fucking"; it was what he thought sex was and what he was supposed to do as a male. "I thought at the time that dominating someone sexually, like a boy smaller than me, was what a male just did. I just learned that from my stepfather." At this time in John's life, homosexual domination was a major resource for "doing masculinity": "That's all I knew. It was all I knew as okay." Indeed, before high school John had developed only a vague understanding of heterosexuality, primarily through the media. It was not until interaction with other teenagers in high school (and "sex ed" class) that John developed a comprehension of heterosexuality. What follows is an extended dialogue disclosing John's initial high school exposure to heterosexuality.

Q. When you were in high school, did you hear about boys who had girlfriends?
   A. Yeah. I heard about that all the time and how they did all this stuff, you know, with the sex stuff. I heard about all that.
Q. How did you respond?
   A. I thought that these guys have girlfriends and I'm sitting here having sex with a young man. That was embarrassing to think about that. And I did think that there was something wrong with me, you know.
Q. Were there gay kids at your school?
   A. No. Not that I knew about. The people at my high school hated gay people; they beat them up and stuff like that. So I couldn't be gay.
Q. They would make comments about gay people?
   A. They'd say they hate gay people, and anytime they'd get their hands on them they're gonna kill 'em and just comments like that.

Q. And you started to think you were gay?

A. Yeah. I started thinking, "Wow, I must be gay or something" because I had sex with a young boy. You know I didn't think of it as rape. You know, I didn't even consider what I was doing as rape.

Q. So interaction at school taught you something new about sexuality?

A. I was gay and I couldn't do that.

Q. You didn't want to be gay?

A. Right. So I stopped having sex with him.

Q. You now wanted to be heterosexual?

A. I didn't want to be sexual with a male, period.

Through interaction in high school John developed a sexual label for his victimization by his stepfather and for his victimizing the neighbor boy—both experiences were now interpreted as "being gay." And because of the negative connotations verbalized at school, John desired exclusive sexual contact with girls. Moreover, this clearly had a gender dimension. According to John, "To be male you have to be sexual with a female." When I asked him where he learned this, John responded, "Because I heard the guys at school talking, you know. I heard the stuff about them having sex with these girls and how they thought it was cool, you know. That's all they talked about, and I wanted to be cool." Accordingly, John attempted to meet several girls at school but was "pushed away." Girls did not pay attention to him and several called him "a geek, a loser." Consequently, he felt unfit to continue asserting himself around girls.

> I was inadequate. I really didn't know what to do, so I didn't make a fool out of myself. So I thought it was better to rape a woman. Plus, if I fucked a woman, I didn't have to feel gay. So, that's what I told myself. I had to start doing something. That's when I started having sex with an older female, my aunt.

John felt that if he was "having sex" with his aunt, he would be "cool." As he expressed this point:

> The guys at school bragged about sex. I felt if I'm gettin' sex with an older female then I'm doing what these guys at school are doing. And so I forced her to perform acts [anal, vaginal, and oral penetration] with me

that she didn't want to do. Deep inside I felt worthless. And you know I felt like a wimp because people at school would put me down. And when I was fucking my aunt I was powerful; I had the control and she was scared of me. I was like, "Wow, this is powerful."

John's aunt was two years older but physically smaller. She would be at his house to clean and cook the evening meal when John came home from school. He now was in the position to use his physical size to control and dominate a woman. When asked why he chose his aunt, John replied, "I picked her because she was shy, quiet, and easy to control, and she was accessible."

Like Sam, John felt powerful when sexually assaulting his aunt (and earlier when sexually assaulting the young neighbor boy). The sexual violence—as a contextually based masculine resource—allowed him to momentarily diminish his negative masculine self-esteem and to feel like a "real man." As John states:

I was like, wow, this is really powerful, and I remember how I felt when I was being teased. So when I was fucking my aunt I was like, this is really powerful and I continued to do it more and more to get that power and control over another person.

I asked John to expand on the following points:

Q. Is that how you felt during the actual violence?

A. When I was actually in the process of doing this, it felt really powerful. The intensity of that power was unreal. But afterwards I didn't feel that power and control anymore. I went back to feeling lousy.

Q. Why did the sexual violence make you feel powerful?

A. Because I was the one in control. I was the one pushing this person around. I was the one who was being listened to and I was the one who they feared.

Q. How did you feel anticipating and planning the abuse?

A. I felt invincible and unstoppable.

Q. Why?

A. Just getting one up over the people I fucked. I got one up over their families because they thought I was this really nice kid, and here I was doing this and I thought I'm untouchable. It was kind of a rush.

Q. When you were planning the sexual violence did you think about getting caught?

A. That was the farthest thing from my mind. I never thought about getting caught, because I felt unstoppable.

Q. So it made you feel special?

A. I just wanted to establish myself that I was really strong and nobody can stop me. Just being that tough guy.

Q. You didn't feel like a tough guy at school?

A. I felt lousy after I came home from school, and I'd fuck my aunt. I'd go to school, feel lousy, come home, and fuck my aunt. And it was just like a cycle.

Q. So the violence had a pleasurable quality to it?

A. It was sexually pleasurable, it had that good feeling. Also, when I was fucking my aunt I didn't feel inadequate anymore because I was having sex, so I couldn't have been an outcast anymore. I'd like have sexual contact with a girl.

Q. So it had a sexual component to it?

A. Yeah. I didn't think about it as violence. I just thought about getting my way, you know. I didn't think about that I was hurting her. That didn't dawn on me.

Q. Was sex something you should have?

A. Yeah. I wanted it just like other guys have it. When I was fucking my aunt, I thought she owes it to me so she should do what I say. It was that ownership way of thinking: "She's mine so she's gonna do what I want her to do." So there were thoughts like that.

Q. Why did your aunt owe it to you?

A. I felt entitled, 'cause I'm a guy.

Until he was fourteen, John conceptualized sexuality as same-sex sexuality—an act older males forced on younger males. With a changing social situation—from junior high to high school—came a differing definition of sexuality and, subsequently, a transformed criteria of maleness. Now sexuality was represented as heterosexuality, and (similar to his earlier sexual assault of the seven-year-old boy) the sexual assault of his aunt became an appropriate contextual resource for doing masculinity. Each act of control, power, and sexual arousal associated with the sexual domination of his aunt convinced John that he was masculine, that he was not an "outcast." This sense of masculinity—like Sam's—lasted only until he went back to school. Because the sexual violence did not resolve the threatening masculine situation at school, John continually faced a lack of masculine resources and therefore continuing masculine self-doubts. Consequently, sexual violence was not a one-time situation but occurred over and over again.

Zack

Zack was a youthful fifteen-year-old who was intrigued about my being interested in his life story. However, the atmosphere was a bit somber and I sensed a smidgen of shame in him for his past behavior. Nevertheless, he quickly immersed himself in conversation.

Zack was from a working-class town where he lived with his grandmother, aunt, uncle, and two younger female cousins (9 and 12 years of age). Zack became a member of this family at age four, when his grandmother adopted him. His biological father disappeared when Zack was two. His mother, an alcoholic, is unable to care for him. The adoption initially was distressing to Zack:

> She [grandmother] came to pick me up and I really didn't want to go. I was really attached to my mom, and I remember just crawling under a table and latching myself to my mom's leg and not wanting to go.
> *Q. You were frightened of moving in with your grandmother?*
> A. Yeah, but my grandmother was real nice to me and she told me why I had to come—that my mom couldn't take care of me.

Both Zack's grandmother and his uncle work in the skilled labor market. His aunt works only at home, where she does most of the household cooking and cleaning. The kids and the uncle have no assigned household chores, except for "helping out" now and then as needed. Besides reporting these explicit practices defining "men's work" and "women's work" at home, Zack's account of family interaction revealed a very close relationship with his grandmother. During Christmas she would always "buy me a room full of toys. It was unbelievable. I really liked her a lot." Zack also described a warm bond with his uncle. In fact, Zack's uncle was his only model of masculinity while he was growing up—his uncle's ideas and practices representing what masculinity "was all about." During the years they lived together, Zack's uncle instilled in him a liking for sport, especially football. Indeed, it was this interaction with his uncle that cultivated Zack's idea of a future: "Since I was young, I wanted to be a football player. I watched football on TV with my uncle all the time and

I'd say, 'Wow, look at that, that's gonna be me someday.' And my uncle would say, 'That's great, Zack.'" It meant a lot to Zack that his uncle approved of his interest in football. Indeed, Zack stated that throughout his childhood the meaning of masculinity remained the same—to "be strong and a good football player. That's it."

Zack did not, however, enjoy such an amiable relationship with his aunt. In fact, she was physically and verbally abusive to Zack but not his two younger cousins. Zack's aunt was extremely obese and would use her size against him—slapping him, pushing him, and throwing him against walls. Zack felt he could never do anything to please his aunt, eventually concluding that he was the cause of the physical violence and verbal abuse: "She would swear at me and say, 'If you weren't such a bad kid I wouldn't have to act like this.' I felt I was the problem, something about me, because she never screamed like that at my cousins, you know."

Thus Zack saw his aunt as having the power in the house and using it in an aggressive and tyrannical manner. His grandmother and uncle were passive members of the family who deferred to his aunt and never disciplined Zack or his cousins: "She controlled everything. My grandmother and uncle just paid the bills and brought in the food. She was like a saint to everyone but me." His relationship with his aunt was extremely distressing to Zack, and participation at school reinforced the negative masculine self-esteem that evolved from this interaction at home.

Initially Zack liked school and did quite well. From kindergarten to second grade Zack "really excelled in school," was "doing awesome" schoolwork, and had lots of friends. However, in third grade circumstances at school began to change. By this time he had gained a considerable amount of weight and other students considered him "fat," as did he himself. As Zack states, "I was really chubby and large, and I wasn't very athletic. I dressed funny. I'd wear sweat pants and the shirts with little alligators—so I wasn't popular." The "cool guys" at school would consistently verbally and physically abuse Zack: "They'd call me 'fatty,' 'chubby cheeks,' 'wimp,' and stuff like that. I got pushed down a lot and stuff. I got beat up a lot in the schoolyard."

The abuse for being overweight and the constant physical assault extended through grade school and middle school. Unlike some other kids at school, Zack did not respond physically to the abuse because he felt he would be "beat up." When asked if he discussed this abuse with anyone at home, Zack replied, "Yeah, I talked with my uncle. I'd come home and say, 'People are picking on me at school,' and he'd say, 'Oh, you have to fight back or they'll keep it up.' But I was scared to fight back. So I was really confused what to do."

Throughout third and fourth grades, Zack coped with the abuse by avoiding, as much as possible, the "popular kids" (who seemed to be doing most of it). In the fifth grade, however, after discussing the abuse with his uncle, Zack decided he would follow the examples at school as well as his uncle's advice because simply avoiding the provoking students was not working. During one major abusive incident in which he was persistently pushed around by a "cool guy," Zack attempted to "fight back" physically but was beaten severely: "He pile drived me into the ground." At the end of the "fight" (which took place on the playground while a large group watched), several students shouted "names at me like 'fatty,' 'fatty can't fight,' 'you're a wimp,' stuff like that." I asked Zack how that made him feel and he answered, "Like I was fat, weird, and a wimp. It really bothered me that kids at school didn't like me."

Thus Zack experienced embarrassment in school for poor grades, feelings of masculine inadequacy because of his physical size and shape, and a sense of masculine powerlessness because of his inability to "do masculinity" in the way his milieu suggested—fighting back. Zack thus became even more of a loner at school, stopped discussing the bullying with his uncle, and never again attempted to respond physically to the harassment. When he came home from school, Zack would not play with other kids ("they wouldn't play with me") and usually locked himself in his room to concentrate on video games. As Zack put it:

> I felt like I was a "wimp" 'cause I couldn't do what other boys did. I never could in my life. I couldn't do anything. Other people always told me what to do, I never told anybody. I felt pretty crappy about myself. I didn't like myself and I couldn't really talk to my uncle about it.

At school Zack, like Sam and John, was defined socially as *embodying* a subordinate masculinity; he endured this characterization and consequently life both at home and at school seemed hopeless to him. Zack did not give up entirely because he was determined to play on the junior high football team, not only because of his love of football but also to show people that he was "somebody":

> It would make me feel like I was actually worth something, like other guys, you know. That I actually had a point to actually do something

that would really be mine, and that was football. I really liked football and because I was big [heavy] maybe I could be a lineman. I never was good at anything but maybe football. My uncle always wanted me to play football and he said I was good at it. Football was something I might be able to cling to—maybe it was something I had above every-body else.

However, during the summer, between fifth and sixth grades, Zack broke his wrist while attempting to "get in shape." He remained over-weight, however, and although he tried out for the team in his sixth-grade year, he was soon cut. Consequently, Zack felt even less secure about his masculinity and apparently so did his classmates: "They contin-ued to make fun of me, call me names and say I couldn't do nothin'." So Zack perpetually avoided his classmates, which was not difficult because he was, in turn, rejected by most of them. According to Zack, the only classmates who would have anything to do with him was a group of boys he called "the misfits." Zack's interaction with the misfits took place only during school lunch: "We'd all sit at the table, and you'd look at us and we'd all look like a bunch of misfits." Otherwise Zack did not "hang out" with other kids: "I wasn't part of any groups." He identified three major groups in school: "The popular kids—the people who were good looking, athletes, had the cool clothes, and the girls. The brains—the people who did good in school. And then—us."

Despite his lack of school friends, during his sixth-grade year Zack de-veloped a sexual interest in girls. He learned this not from the adults at home but through interaction at school. As Zack states:

Me and the other misfits at the lunch table talked about sex and stuff. We'd see a girl sitting in the lunchroom and we'd say, 'Have you heard about her? She's pretty nice.' And then we'd just talk about her and some girls that we liked and stuff. What kind of reputation she had, what we thought about her. Nothing too gross or out of line, you know. Other than that, I didn't have any sexuality.

While the misfits were restrained in their discussions of sexuality at the lunch table, the popular kids were boisterous: "They talked about it all the time. They talked about it a lot more at their table. They'd be right out loud about it, talking about 'getting laid,' and oral sex, and stuff. They al-ways bragged about having a lot of sex and stuff."

Because of the frequent "sex talk" at school, Zack wanted to experience sex to be like all the other boys. Many popular boys and some of the "misfits" had allegedly engaged in intercourse, so Zack felt extremely "left out," especially since he had never been able to arrange a date. He identified himself as a "virgin," a status other boys—including numerous "misfits"—had long ago surpassed.

> There were some girls that I asked out and they said, 'I'm not really ready for a relationship.' I knew that was a crock. You know how girls sometimes make excuses because they don't want to go out with you. And I knew the truth was that they didn't want to go out with me because I was fat and not good looking or something like that.

The continuing rejection by girls made Zack feel discontented: "I didn't really like myself 'cause girls didn't like me. I was fat and I just didn't seem to fit in. Like I'm the only virgin in the school."

Q. Did you want to fit in?
 A. Yeah. And I tried really hard. I tried to play football so the popular guys would like me. I tried to dress differently, dress like they [popular kids] did. I tried going on diets. I tried to get girls.
Q. You wanted to be accepted into the popular crowd?
 A. Right. But they didn't want anything to do with me. My size, and I just didn't have the looks that they did, you know. The only way that you are in the popular group is that you have to be good at sports and girls have to like you. And I was bad at sports and girls hated me.

By age eleven, Zack endured serious and continuous forms of abuse at school regarding his physical size and shape. Rather than accept his body as something personal and unique, Zack attempted to "fit in" by adopting certain situationally normative masculine practices: fighting back, playing football, dressing "cool," and obtaining heterosexual dates. He failed miserably at each and had no one with whom to discuss this terribly bothersome situation. Moreover, this is exactly the time (age 11) when he learned from his grandmother that no one in his family, except her, had been interested in adopting him when he was four years old: "My grandmother told me that my mom called everyone in my family and said, 'Can you take my son?' And they all said no. And my grandmother was the only one that said yes." Asked how that made him feel, Zack

replied, "I felt real bad about myself. I thought there must really be something wrong with me 'cause no one wants me, you know." Cumulatively,
all these facts presented a serious lack of masculine resources and consequently a lack of masculine self-esteem at home and at school: "I wasn't
happy at home and I wasn't happy at school. I couldn't do anything right
and everybody thought I was a misfit. I didn't want to be a misfit and
needed something to cheer me up."

Accordingly, like Sam and John, Zack sought to overcome his lack of
masculine resources—and therefore his low masculine self-esteem—
through controlling and dominating behaviors involving the use of sexual
power. Unable to be masculine like the "cool guys" and terribly degraded
at home, Zack turned to an available masculine practice—expressing control and power over his youngest female cousin through sexuality. During
his sixth-grade year—a time when he experienced the distressing events
just described and "discovered" heterosexuality—Zack sought out his
cousin: "I wanted to experience sex, like what other boys were doing. I
wanted to do what they were talking about but I was rejected by girls at
school." I asked Zack to elaborate on why he turned to his youngest cousin:

> It was in the sixth grade. Me and my younger cousin, who was six at the
> time, we started to play this game Truth or Dare. And we just dared each
> other to do something. It started out pretty normal, just like standing on
> your head and stuff like that. But it just progressed into sexual stuff, un-
> til it was just sexual contact like oral sex and touching and stuff like that.
> *Q. Your cousin just went along with the game?*
>   A. Not the sexual stuff. She'd say, "No, I don't really want to," and
> then I'd force her into it.
> *Q. How did you force her?*
>   A. Like I'd say, "Oh, I'll let you play my Sega," because I had a Sega
> and she used to always want to come and play.
> *Q. Then she would agree to do what you asked?*
>   A. Yeah. It started out with her just touching over my clothing, and
> then it progressed to taking off each other's clothes and touching each
> other and stuff like that.
> *Q. And she never questioned it?*
>   A. No, not anymore, 'cause I always let her play my Sega.

Zack sexually assaulted (fondling and oral penetration) his youngest
cousin over a three-year period (until he was 14 and she was 9) by using

the manipulative strategy described. The following dialogue reveals what the sexual violence accomplished for Zack:

Q. How did it make you feel when you were able to manipulate your cousin?

A. It made me feel real good. I just felt like finally I was in control over somebody. I forgot about being fat and ugly. She was someone looking up to me, you know. If I needed sexual contact, then I had it. I wasn't a virgin anymore.

Q. Is that why you sexually assaulted your cousin for three years?

A. Yeah. I wanted control over something in my life, and this gave it to me. I finally felt like one of the guys.

Q. What were you thinking about right before you sexually assaulted your cousin?

A. I was just really down because I had a rough day at school.

Q. What do you mean by "a rough day"?

A. Just a lot of teasing, being called names and being pushed around a lot. Not having any friends that meant anything. Kind of depressed about school. Not able to do things like everybody else. That made me sad.

Q. Then you would come home from school and play the game with your cousin?

A. Yeah. And that would cheer me up, make me feel better. Plus I would be sexually satisfied 'cause she would masturbate me and give me blow jobs and feeling like I have affection. No one ever said good things about me and I never did things that the other guys did. But now I did, and it was really cool.

Q. Why did you choose your youngest cousin?

A. 'Cause I could tell that she was more accessible and just really easy to be able to take advantage of. She always aimed to please everyone else, so I took advantage of that. And if I let her play Sega, she wouldn't tell anybody.

Q. Did you ever talk about this with the misfits or other kids at school?

A. No. But I could now talk about sex with them if I had to. I knew what it looked like and how it felt now, that kind of thing. So I felt I fit in more.

Zack, like John, experienced traumatic and emotionally difficult interactions in his family and at school. The lack of masculine self-esteem developed at home was reinforced by his inability to be masculine at school. Consequently, the control, power, and sexual arousal associated with the sexual domination of his youngest cousin provided Zack a contextually based masculine resource when other masculine resources were unavailable—he was now a "cool guy." The sexual violence provided a sense of masculine accomplishment and therefore heightened his masculine self-esteem. However, as with Sam and John, the sense of maleness derived from this violent practice was short-lived, lasting usually only until Zack returned to school. Because the sexual violence did not resolve the persistently threatening masculine situation at home and school, Zack repeatedly faced a lack of masculine resources and therefore self-doubts, which explains his continuing achievement of masculinity through his ongoing sexual assault of his younger cousin.

Conclusion

The sex offender life histories show that each boy's relationship with parent or guardian differed. Sam experienced a nonviolent and affectionate relationship with both parents; John suffered verbal, physical, and sexual violence from his stepfather and had an unreliable mother; and Zack endured physical and verbal violence from his aunt but had a warm relationship with his uncle and grandmother. Moreover, each boy had different masculine interests—from working with tools to carpentry to football. Nevertheless, at home all three boys appropriated a definition of masculinity that also emphasized the use of physical violence as the ultimate resolution to interpersonal problems.

At school, all three boys were often the victims of peer abuse because of their physical size and shape and for not being "a man"—they did not "fight back" as their social milieu suggested they should. Each accepted the notion that being masculine meant responding to provocation with physical violence, but because each was physically small and/or obese in relation to the boys perpetrating the abuse, they felt unable to respond in such a "manly" fashion. Significantly, all three boys were unable to discuss with any adult at home their unsettling masculine situation at school. Simultaneously, each of the boys recounted adopting heterosexuality through interaction at school. Sam and Zack considered themselves heterosexual virgins who wanted to experience "sex like the guys" because this is what "every guy does"; John initially identified sex as same-sex sexuality yet he changed his sexual orientation once he entered high school because "to be male you have to be sexual with a female." However, all three boys were unable to secure heterosexual relationships. Thus

Sam, John, and Zack found themselves in the social situation of the school that defined both physical and sexual performance as essential criterion for "doing masculinity." Yet it was their inability to construct such masculine notions at school and their perceptions of alternative sexual opportunities at home that directed their ultimate choice of sexual violence. In short, the three sex offenders attempted to invalidate their subordinate masculine status at school through a personal reconstruction of masculinity at home. For Sam, John, and Zack, the common denominator consisted not of abuse by family members at home but abuse by peers at school, the inability to physically "fight back" against such abuse, and the emphasis on (yet inability to "do") heterosexuality.

In the public arenas of junior high school and high school, Sam, John, and Zack were powerless in masculine terms; after school, in the private, isolated setting at home, they were powerful. Indeed, their agency constituted discovering such a powerful site—the space, time, and form of interaction to "become real men." Sexual violence was the perceived available resource summoned by each boy because, quite simply, each lacked other contextual resources with which to accomplish gender according to the situationally defined criteria at school. Sam, John, and Zack applied the dominant contextual ideals of masculinity to the situations that faced them. And in the brief, illusory moment of each sexually violent incident, Sam, John, and Zack were the "cool guys," the subordinate was the dominant. They were now "real men."

Let us now turn our attention to the assaultive boys.

3
Hugh, Perry, and Lenny

In this chapter I present the life stories of Hugh (age 15), Perry (age 17), and Lenny (age 15). All three boys, in different ways, were involved in assaultive offending. Hugh and Perry developed a "tough guy" masculinity whereas Lenny—initially defined by others as a "wimp"—restructured his conduct to present himself, likewise, as a "tough guy." Lenny grew up in a nonviolent home whereas Hugh and Perry experienced a violent and conflictual family environment. These three life stories are analytically compared and contrasted, allowing opportunities to investigate different family and school relations and their connections to assaultive offending. These life stories, like the ones in Chapter 2, advance the literature on assaultive violence through comparisons of changing masculinities and involvement in assault throughout the life course. Let's begin with Hugh.

Hugh

Hugh was a tall, well-built fifteen-year-old male who was full of excitement about telling me his life story. He presented a confident and bold demeanor and seemed to enjoy discussing the various circumstances he had experienced in his short life.

Among Hugh's most vivid childhood memories was his mother's death in a car accident, which occurred when he was two. He later learned that the driver of the car was his *inebriated father*. Subsequently, Hugh and his younger (by one year) sister were adopted by their grandparents. Hugh lived with his grandparents for the next ten years, until he was twelve. According to Hugh, this event bothered him when he was a young boy—"I wanted a real mom and dad"—but eventually he "got over it."

Both "Gram" and "Gramps" (as he calls them) worked at factory jobs and were never at home when Hugh left for school. During elementary and junior high school, Hugh and his sister made their own breakfast and walked to school together. According to Hugh, the only thing the "family" did together was go camping: "They'd like to go camping, so they took my sister and me. But they didn't like to do any of the other things I liked to do." Hugh emphasized that the only "other thing" the family did together was "work on chores." Saturday was designated "chore day." Hugh's chores included cleaning his room, raking leaves, mowing the lawn, shoveling snow, and helping Gramps fix things around the house. Hugh's sister cleaned her room and was responsible for doing the dishes, vacuuming, and helping Gram with the laundry. Hugh, then, grew up among explicit practices defining "men's work" and "women's work" at home.

During the ten years he lived with his grandparents, Hugh reports a very warm relationship with Gram: "It was always good with my Gram." But he had a difficult relationship with Gramps: "We kind of had this thing. I never got along with him. I couldn't handle him being there. I always thought he was a mean guy." For example, Gram never spanked Hugh for misbehavior but Gramps did. He was a big man and would sometimes hit Hugh with a "switch." The spankings "made me hate my grandfather. He was so controlling; never let me do anything I wanted and always hit me when I did wrong." Hugh saw his grandfather as an extremely domineering man who never allowed him to do "kids' stuff," such as "sleep over at other kids' houses. [He] didn't let me go to school dances. I always had to leave a note whenever I went somewhere when they were at work. If I didn't I would get hit with the switch."

So Hugh grew up with a patriarchal grandfather who frequently wielded his power: "Gramps told everybody what to do, my Gram too," and Hugh interpreted his home situation as "being his slave." Moreover, Hugh's grandfather never seemed to spend time with him: "I never had a father to play catch with, go fishing; my Gramps hated that stuff." Hugh's initial model of masculinity, Gramps, thus emphasized manual labor inside (fixing things) and outside (factory work) the home, as well as male power in the household.

As a young boy, Hugh was also involved in fighting. He remembers Gramps emphasizing to him that "it was okay" to participate in physical violence if Hugh was "picked on" by bigger kids, "so I used to get in fights when I was just a little kid." Classmates his age and close neighborhood friends never harassed Hugh. At school, however, older boys frequently attempted to dominate and control him. For example, on the playground of the grade school older boys occasionally would "try to kick us off the field because they wanted to play kick ball and I would say: 'We were here first.' And they would tell us to get off and I'd take a swing at them. It was always my way of solving stuff." Hugh talked with Gramps about these confrontations with the older boys and Gramps endorsed his physically fighting back:

> That's about the only thing he was proud of me for. He would say: "Did you lick the other kid?" And I'd say, "Yeah." And he'd say, "That's my boy." That's the only time he was happy. He always made sure it was a equal fight. It was not okay with him if I beat up a kid smaller than me. They had to be on the same plane. I only fought older kids. The older kids, they'd say things to provoke stuff, you know. You know how older kids always pick on little kids? So whenever they started to pick on us, I would fight back. I could hold my own.

The following dialogue reflects his classmates' response to Hugh's conduct as well as the masculine meaning and image Hugh constructed through the practice of fighting:

> *Q. What did the other kids think about you fighting?*
>
> A. Since I was a good fighter, everybody my age looked up to me, you know. I wasn't afraid to fight. I liked it. I was the only one my age who fought the older kids.
>
> *Q. How did that make you feel?*
>
> A. Better than the others.
>
> *Q. Why?*
>
> A. Always, ever since I can remember, I'd say I wasn't going to let anybody push me around. I was going to be like Gramps said—a force in this world.
>
> *Q. Did you want to be like Gramps? Was he a force?*
>
> A. Yeah. He didn't let people push him around.
>
> *Q. Did the other kids think of you as a force?*
>
> A. They looked up to me, as I said. Because it wasn't about beating the older kids up or them beating me up. It was that I held my own. I didn't let people walk all over me. And they thought that was cool.

Q. Did you develop a reputation?

A. Yeah. I became that force, you know. In the back of kids' minds it would always be like, "Man, is this kid going to hit me?" So they didn't mess with me. I was strong and good with my fists, you know.

Although at school Hugh was a "force" among his classmates, he never liked school and did not do well at schoolwork. He especially disliked teachers who were, for him, "a form of authority." In particular, Hugh detested being told to complete his homework. In fact Hugh never did any homework yet was always passed to the next grade. This circumstance prompted Hugh to laugh (during the interview); at the time it actually took place it provided Hugh a means with which to question the entire educational project. "School was a joke. The only reason they moved me up to the next grade was because they didn't want to deal with me anymore, you know. And that was what happened a lot."

Early in grade school Hugh was bothered that teachers had more power than he did. But after he discovered the physical power he could exert on the playground, he felt confident challenging a teacher's power in the classroom. In particular, when a teacher pressed Hugh to do his schoolwork, he would respond by "acting out in class." I asked Hugh for an example:

The teacher told me to do my work and I'd say: "I don't want to do my work." And then the teacher would say I had to, and then I'd throw my desk at him. I couldn't stay in class and do what I had to do. I was always getting in trouble. I was the one getting detention and stuff. I'd throw my desk and walk out, sayin' "fuck you."

Hugh began throwing desks in elementary school and continued in junior high. When I asked Hugh how it made him feel to respond that way, he stated,

It felt good. It was a sense of retaliation, you know. I was doing something about it. And after I got out of the principal, kids would pat me on the back. They all wanted to be my friend, you know. I had a reputation of not being pushed around by teachers, and I liked that. So I did it more.

Thus Hugh physically controlled what he interpreted as a bad and meaningless social environment. Throughout elementary school and junior high he defined his masculinity against the school and its overall project.

At school Hugh's physical presence allowed him to be part of what he called "the tough crowd." He hung out with other boys who had a "tough" reputation. They participated occasionally in physical violence on the playground, "fighting kids who got in our way," and they would also verbally and physically abuse the "wimps" and "nerds." As Hugh put it:

We couldn't stand the wimps and nerds, the fat and ugly kids. They just sit there and do the homework and shit like that. We'd trip them in the hall, knock 'em on the side of the head, punch them, throw food at 'em in the lunch room, and stuff like that. They're just wimps and worthless. It was fun 'cause they couldn't do anything to us, you know. We liked to do shit like that to them 'cause they'd just let us do it. It made the time at school fun, you know.

Other than "acting out," abusing the "wimps," and fighting, the only other thing Hugh liked about school was sports. In grade school and junior high Hugh played all sports but he especially liked baseball and soccer. When he was in the fifth grade Hugh was the junior high MVP for soccer, "cause I could run fast, and when I learned how to handle the ball, you know—that's all it took." As such, Hugh was accepted into the "popular group" because of his athletic ability. However, his tough and physical presence outside the sports arena tended to marginalize him from this group and consequently strengthened his attachment to the "tough crowd."

Not surprisingly, Hugh's hero during junior high was the professional football and baseball player Bo Jackson. Hugh owned a complete set of his baseball cards and had a poster of Bo on his bedroom wall. When I asked him why Bo Jackson, Hugh responded:

Cause he did it, you know. He did what he wanted, you know. He didn't let people push him around and he played two sports. Strong man. That's what I wanted to be like.

It was also during his fifth- and sixth-grade years that Hugh experienced a sexual awakening. He was introduced to sex through pornography that Gramps kept at home (magazines were available on the coffee table). I asked Hugh if he had any sexual interaction at school and he responded that "lots of people had boyfriends and girlfriends but I didn't. When I was in school, I didn't care about sex, never thought of it much. Just wanted to play sports, you know, and fuck around with my friends."

Thus throughout elementary school and junior high Hugh was a "cool guy" because he participated in sports and in this way developed a physical presence in school. He enjoyed a reputation for being tough and was rewarded with friendship from other boys because of his physicality, his degradation and subordination of the "wimps," and his success on the athletic field. Additionally, Hugh was admired by many kids for progressing through school without any effort—he "beat the system." In short, Hugh literally rose above many other boys in school, thereby constructing a specific type of in-school exemplary masculinity.

However, because of his "acting out" in the classroom, abusing other kids, and continued fighting on the playground, Hugh was eventually barred from participating in school sports. Hugh felt ill-treated and wounded by this edict and realized that his "cool" masculinity was lost: "That was it for me. I hated school more and it was then I decided to leave, get out of school." School no longer "made sense" to his future plans. As far as Hugh was concerned, now that he was no longer allowed to participate in school sports he would never be another Bo Jackson: "I would probably end up like Gram and Gramps, a stupid factory worker." Hugh soon decided he had had enough "authority" at home and school. The authoritarianism at school and home, combined with the overall meaninglessness of school ("who needs an education to work in a factory?"), led him to drop out of school. As Hugh put it:

> I needed to do what I wanted to do. It's just that I wanted to be free of any rule, you know. I didn't want anybody telling me what to do. I'm not a girl, you know [laughter]. I wanted to get away from home and school rules. So I went out and met these people, and came down with them and started living their life.

When Hugh was only twelve (in seventh grade), he dropped out of school (never to return) and began to run the streets, eventually meeting some boys who were members of a gang. Hugh was attracted to the street life and the males he met there because, as he put it, "They are like Bo Jackson, you know. They 'beat the system.'" He would be gone from his grandparents' home for months at a time, and then "I'd come back home and Gramps would hassle me to go back to school, and I'd run off again."

When Hugh "ran off" he would usually share an apartment with a member of the gang. I asked Hugh what he liked about the gang:

> They were like me. They didn't like society's rules. Even the rich people don't follow rules so-why-should-we kind of thing, you know. And they have my back and stuff. If I needed it, they'd have my back. If I had a problem, they'd have my back and I had their back if they had a problem and we'd always do stuff together. We would just chill, do drugs, you know.

Hugh found a collective identity in the gang, a new venue that was more amicable and inviting because it provided a feeling of belonging that was unavailable to him at school or at home. Hugh described a normal day for a gang member:

> Like chilling in the apartment. Like hanging out in the apartment, smoking blunts. If we had money, getting a line. If we didn't have the money, we'd just rob people. We'd like rob houses and we'd like go downtown, swing by and grab a purse or just hit someone and grab a purse or wallet. It was like two or three of us doing it.

With the money they obtained from robbery and burglary, Hugh and his boys bought food, clothes, and "sacks of crack." They would sell half the sack and smoke the rest. In addition to the economic benefit, Hugh participated in robbery and burglary because "it was to be part of the crew, you know. It was just about being part of the crew and getting, you know, getting your face, getting your respect from your boys."

Gang participation required frequent involvement in assaultive violence. Hugh described many assaults, all of which were perpetrated by either individuals or the group. Hugh provided this example of an individual assault:

> I was at this dance club with my boys and girlfriend. There was this kid inside who was talking shit to us, talking shit to my girlfriend. So I said, "Let's go outside" because I don't want him talking shit. And so we go outside and I say, "Man, why you talking shit to me and my girl?" And he said nothin', just standin' there given me that look, you know. And I have all my boys on my back; there were like eight, nine guys behind me, you know. And then I exploded on him. I punched him like three

times, and he fell on the ground and he didn't even try to get back up. I pulled a pair of brass knuckles out of my pocket and I just started waling on him, crushed the side of his face. I put him in the hospital.

Q. What did he say to you when he was "talking shit"?

A. He called my girlfriend a "bitch" and me a "punk."

Q. So that bothered you?

A. Yeah. She ain't a "bitch" and I ain't a "punk," and I showed him who the "punk" is.

Although Hugh had "his boys" behind him, this was an "individual" assault because he alone was responsible to settle the dispute physically. His boys would have participated only if the opponent had help from others. When I asked Hugh why he engaged in this physical violence, he stated:

To hold my respect with my boys. I had all the boys behind me, hearing this kid talk shit. If I'd just left it alone, it would go into their heads that I don't deserve their respect. If I can't even hold my respect for myself how can I hold it from them?

Group violence differed. Every day Hugh and his boys (and girls) would smoke marijuana, cocaine, and/or crack, and then the whole gang would either go out to a club or "go stomping" (controlling their "territory" through violence).

Q. Is stomping also about holding your respect?

A. Yeah. You do it to be one of the boys. It's loyalty to the boys and to our territory. It's holding on to what's ours, you know. We stomp to show our loyalty to each other and to show our territory.

Q. Describe for me a stomping.

A. My boys would be strapped [have guns]. I would be strapped. Someone would have a knife, you know. If we find dudes in our territory we jump out the car and start to beat on 'em. If people start shooting, you have to shoot back. More people get hurt, but you save yourself, you know. The more you can take out of them, the less people on your side get hurt.

For Hugh, then, both types of assaultive violence were masculine practices. Indeed, when asked what it meant to be masculine at ages twelve to fifteen (the peak years of Hugh's gang involvement), Hugh responded that he and the other boys were expected to be "strong, be able to hold your own, be able to fight, not back down when someone is in your face. It's just like not show fear. You can't show fear when you are a man."

Although girls were also in the gang and at times were involved in stomping (fighting the girls in the other gang), the major difference between males and females was, according to Hugh, "We had the power. We told them what to do." The following is an extended dialogue on gendered power in Hugh's gang:

Q. Can you further explain that?

A. You know, we'd all help cook and clean the apartment and shit like that, guys and girls together. But if a girl talk trash to you or if a girl was like running a mouth to you, we wouldn't have it. She'd just get slapped down till she wouldn't know where she was.

Q. It's okay to "slap down" girls in the gang?

A. Oh yeah, if they get out of hand.

Q. How often did that occur?

A. It wasn't like everyday because they knew who they were and they knew what they had to do, you know. They knew where they stood and they knew where we stood.

Q. Is "slapping a girl down" a form of violence?

A. No, it's not violence because violence is not the way it should be. When you keep a girl in check, that's the way it should be. If she talks shit and you slap her down, that would not be violence.

Q. Is it ever appropriate to have sex with a girl if she does not want to?

A. No, that's not right. We'd bust them out if they did that. Once we heard about a kid who raped his sister, so we went and found him and broke both his arms. There was like bone coming out. We fucked him up bad. That just don't happen, you know. We don't like rapists.

Q. When is violence against women appropriate?

A. Women should get respect from men unless they deserve to lose that respect.

Q. What would cause a woman to lose that respect?

A. Like being a bitch, talking shit. But then they wouldn't get raped, you know. They'd just get slapped down and told to shut the fuck up and get out of the house.

Although Hugh learned about sex at home through Gramps's pornography and at school through the "sex talk" of other boys, he remained celibate until thirteen when he was a member of the gang. Hugh had several girlfriends in the gang, and during these "gang years" sexuality took on a heightened meaning in his life. I asked Hugh to describe sexual relations in the gang:

> It works like this. A girl who's with somebody in the gang—it's only him. Then there is the hood rat and she's with everybody. That's how it works. If you got someone, everybody knows to keep their hands off. If they don't, they get fucked up by the gang.
> *Q. What do you mean by "hood rat"?*
> A. There is usually four or five of them. They just go with anybody, with everybody, except for the ones that are taken, you know.
> *Q. What happens if a guy has a girlfriend and then has sex with a hood rat?*
> A. Then the hood rat is going to get busted out. It's just the hood rat, not the guy.

Sexuality is an extremely important part of the gang. According to Hugh, this is so because "to get respect from your boys you gotta have a woman. It's either have one woman all the time or have lots of women. If you can hustle the girls, hustle the money, and hold your own, that's where you get your respect."

> *Q. What about homosexuality?*
> A. Gays aren't accepted in our group.
> *Q. Why not?*
> A. We don't like 'em. We don't think it's right. It's not natural.
> *Q. Did your gang ever bash gays?*
> A. Oh yeah, we stomp 'em all the time. We just see them walking down the street and so we stomp 'em because we don't want them in our territory.

During his first fifteen years Hugh was rewarded with favorable appraisal from others for his physicality—at home from Gramps, at school from other kids, in the gang from "his boys." Although Hugh had a traumatic and emotionally difficult family life, he did not perceive his adoption as his responsibility and he was able to satisfy Gramps's masculine criteria of "fighting back." Indeed, Hugh practiced masculine power and control both at school (over other kids and teachers) and in the street. Hugh used his physical resource—and its accompanying positive masculine self-esteem—to dominate others through assaultive violence. Hugh responded physically when others attempted to challenge his masculinity ("talking shit"), and physical confrontation with "enemy warriors" was an essential criteria for active gang membership.

Perry

Perry had the physical appearance that many revere in teenage boys—he was tall, dark, and handsome. He presented a calm and cool persona, and his direct and self-assured style suggested greater sophistication than most seventeen-year-olds possess.

Perry's earliest family memory was of his biological parents' constant arguing. Their conflictual relationship increased when his father lost his job. "Money problems" became an issue and subsequently both parents became heavy drinkers. Each quarrel ended with Perry's father physically assaulting his mother. When Perry was four years old, his parents divorced and Perry lived alone with his mother, never seeing his father again.

Following the divorce, living with mother was fun for Perry because she stopped drinking and began to "spoil" him by providing money and toys when he wanted; she did not require that he perform any household chores. Perry recounted one of his most memorable activities with his mother:

> On her days off and on the weekends, it was like a tradition to go out and eat and go shopping, to go and see relatives. Every Sunday we'd go and see my grandmother, and we would go out to eat and visit for a while.

Perry's mom worked full-time in the unskilled service sector of the economy; Perry always looked forward to her coming home. Perry had a very close relationship with his mother and found it "really easy to talk to her about things." Whenever he experienced problems, "It felt good to talk to my mom about it." When Perry misbehaved his mother always sat down with him and they both talked it out—there never was yelling or corporal punishment.

When Perry was seven years old, his mother remarried and his life changed dramatically: "The stepfather was real nice to me when they were dating but when he came into the house he kind of laid down the law. He was the authority figure and I didn't always get what I wanted." Perry's stepfather "had all the power" and "my mom didn't really have any say in anything that went on in the house." Moreover, the stepfather brought his two children (ages 2 and 4) to live with Perry and his mother.

At first Perry was "really excited" about having a younger brother and sister. However, his stepfather always seemed touchy and quick-tempered when Perry was around his new siblings:

> Like I get yelled at and screamed at for the littlest things I did, you know, like laughing at a TV show while my brother and sister are sleeping. He gave me this 'gung-ho' attitude. He was real strict. I got grounded all the time.

The stepfather would not let Perry "hang out" with certain friends. He now received an allowance (if he did his chores) instead of money when he wanted it. And Perry was required to "do the dishes, vacuum all the rooms, pick up messes and stuff like that. Plus, homework had to be done right after I got home from school." Overall, Perry saw his stepfather as a distant and uncaring patriarchal presence who did very little around the house: "My mom and me did all the cleaning and stuff."

A lot of the arguments between the stepfather and Perry began when the stepfather came home from work (he worked in the skilled labor market):

> If he'd had a bad day at work he would just come up and start saying stuff to me, and I would say something back, and then the argument usually would lead to something real physical—like he'd throw me around. He was never really like that to my mother, brother, and sister— never.

His stepfather was in a "bad mood" three or four times a week, so there were frequent verbal and physical confrontations between the two. Thus Perry's early models of masculinity (both his biological father and his stepfather) emphasized male power in the home as a masculine characteristic. Additionally, his stepfather's physically violent response to disagreements validated interpersonal violence as an appropriate masculine method of solving problems.

Despite this troubled home life, Perry had many neighborhood friends with whom he spent considerable time playing:

I was always out with all my friends playing football, basketball, and we'd get real big organized games going on. They were like my second family. Perry spent as much time as possible with his friends because it was fun and I didn't see my stepfather.

Perry loved sports when growing up and had visions of playing in the National Football League. Interested in all sports, he especially liked football. He was a starting lineman on the junior high football team and did much better schoolwork during football season. Moreover, his room was filled with "sports stuff":

My room was loaded. I had football posters on my ceiling, on my walls, on my door. I had a basketball hoop that was a big net to hold my dirty clothes. I had everything, football lamps, you name it.

Perry was very close to his uncle:

When my stepfather and my mother got married, my uncle was kind of like a father figure. He'd take me out of the house and stuff. We did a lot of things that my stepfather wouldn't do for me.
Q. What kinds of things did you do with your uncle?
A. Play basketball, play football, and do all the things my stepfather didn't do. He'd take me fishing. He'd take me out to eat, buy me clothes, buy me toys. He'd take me out of the house as much as he could. He was a really great guy.
Q. You liked to spend time with your uncle?
A. Yeah. It was a good thing to see him and I felt real close to him. I really cared about him. And he liked me. He always said I was good at sports, a natural. That made me feel good inside.
Q. Did you learn anything special from your uncle?
A. He was the one that first got me started thinking about sex. He had these ornaments, car fresheners, and I always used to laugh at them, you know, being naked women on the front of it. And he'd say, "Do you have girlfriends?' And I'd say "No," that I wasn't really interested in girls. And then he would tell me all about sex. He talked a lot about it. He didn't tell me to use rubbers and stuff. He just told me about getting a hard-on and what you do with girls, and that I would like to do it with girls. We made bets on it.

Q. What were the bets?

A. On when I would get laid. How old I would be.

Q. Did you ever talk to your mother or stepfather about sex?

A. My mom never said a thing. My stepfather just was always reminding me when I was going somewhere to have a rubber. If I was going to go screw girls or going to meet girls.

Q. That's all he said?

A. That's it. But my uncle talked to me a lot about sex.

Perry also discussed with his uncle the ongoing distressful relationship with his stepfather. He told him how his stepfather hit him and pushed him around the house:

Q. What did your uncle say?

A. He said he knew about that and that he and my stepfather got into a fight a couple of times over him hitting me. That made me feel good. I felt that someone cared. My mother never stood up for me, but my uncle did.

Q. Were you unable to talk with your mother?

A. More and more my mom started to side with my stepfather. They both yelled at me all the time. When he came into the house, my mom and me was not close anymore.

Q. When your uncle stood up for you did that teach you anything?

A. I got the impression from my uncle getting into fights with my stepfather that it was the right thing to do. Doing this kind of thing was the right thing 'cause I saw this guy that you really looked up to doing that.

Q. He taught you about violence?

A. Yeah, of course. If someone's fucking with you or fucking with someone close to you, you kick their ass. I learned that from my uncle.

Q. Was your uncle an important model in your life?

A. Yeah. He was a great guy. I wanted to be like him 'cause he didn't put up with any shit from anybody.

In school Perry did reasonably well up through sixth grade: "I was getting As and Bs, doing really good in my classes, getting really good comments from my teachers and that really felt good inside." Perry liked his teachers, felt comfortable talking to them, and enjoyed school. He had many friends and loved participating in organized school sports.

In the seventh grade, however, Perry began getting into trouble at school. Sometimes he would "fool around" in class by hassling other students and teachers too. As Perry stated, "I kind of lived for showing off in front of my friends. You know, we would kind of show off in front of each other and we kind of lived for that." Asked what he did in class to "show off," Perry stated he would

> smack a kid in the face or steal his books or misplace something of his, rip up his homework. I would make some kid in class look like a fool, you know. Everybody in the class would be laughing, and I felt good about that.

He engaged in this type of conduct up through the eighth grade: "I was constantly getting suspended from school. My stepfather didn't like that and was getting more angry." Indeed, Perry attributes "home life" as primarily causing his changed attitude toward school. For example, early in the fall of his seventh-grade year Perry fought with his stepfather physically because he was growing much bigger and, as he states, "I wanted to show him like my uncle did":

> I was upstairs in my room listening to some rap music rather loud, and he came in and said he couldn't hear himself think. So I went to turn my stereo down and he kicked a hole in my speaker. I was like, "What the hell did you do that for? Why did you have to be an asshole?" Then he just turned around and snickered and punched me in the face. And I pushed him into my stereo system, and it fell down and a big rack fell on top of him. And he got up, busted my stereo, destroyed all my CDs, and I ran downstairs to the kitchen. He chased me and I grabbed a knife and held it up to him, and I was like, "Hey, back off." He rushed me. I knocked him to the floor and then ran to a friend's house. The cops came and arrested me—not my stepfather.

Being larger physically gave Perry the confidence to stand up against his stepfather. And it felt good to finally retaliate physically. For quite some time Perry had wanted to "hit" his stepfather—especially after learning from his close mentor (uncle) that such a response was legitimate and preferred—but he had always been relatively small. Now, as Perry put it, "I was bigger, and it felt good to knock him down. It was my turn to get physical and I did and it felt real good."

Perry was also using his "growth spurt" to be involved in frequent fights at school. A typical fight scenario went as follows:

Most of the time it was a kid who would get real mouthy and get cocky, and he would have this real tough-guy attitude. I usually started by hitting these little wimps, trying to look tough—where I was the biggest—and usually the fights stopped right there. I'd start and finish it.

Perry gained the status of "school bully" for his behavior: "Usually not too many people would come my way looking for trouble, but if they did they were trying to prove something. They were trying to get my status. But they got their ass kicked instead."

Q. Other kids looked up to you?

A. Yeah. I was a football player and the school bully. People jumped when I moved. Everyone wanted to be my friend.

Q. Were there different cliques in your school?

A. Yeah. There was the smart kids. There was the quiet, ugly, and dumb kids who everyone looked down on 'cause they was wimps. And there was us, the athletes, party animals.

Q. Were you a "cool guy" in school?

A. In some ways. In my friends' eyes. The real "cool guys" was the smart ones that played sports. We played sports, partied, and kicked ass. Everyone was afraid of us.

Q. Did you and your friends talk about sex?

A. Yeah, like who had the biggest breasts, who was the loosest, who gave the best head, who screwed the best.

Q. Was having sex important to you and your friends?

A. Of course. All my friends got laid all the time, and I remember when they said, "We're going to get Perry a fuck tonight."

Q. Tell me about that experience.

A. My first experience was at a party. There was this friend—a really good friend of mine—and he'd have these big parties and have a lot of girls at his house, and everybody would be getting something. So I was thirteen years old and I had gone to this party. And I was already drinking and doing all that stuff, and doing drugs. And it kinda surprised me. I found out after that my friend sent this girl over and we started to fool around with each other, and then the situation kinda having us getting the groove on, you know. And that was the first time I ever had sex.

After this first sexual experience, Perry frequently engaged in intercourse. Indeed, it was a major part of his group interaction at school. Although the teachers did not know of Perry's sexual exploits, he was suspended from school after each physical fight, and when he returned to school he would almost immediately get into another fight. Ultimately, he assaulted teachers as well. Once he attacked a teacher because "he was trying to intimidate me. He was getting in my face, giving me glances." Perry was suspended for that assault; eventually he was expelled for the following incident:

> I was like being vulgar to the teacher, and when he got mad I told him to "suck it." And he told me to get out of class. And once out in the hall he cornered me and started yelling at me. Once he got too close I just like smashed him, and he kind of like bounced off the wall and kind of fell down. And that's when three or four teachers grabbed me and brought me up to the office.
>
> Q. *Did you like any of your teachers?*
> A. No. They were always trying to lay down the law. I didn't like them in my face, trying to confront me.
> Q. *What did your classmates think of your behavior in class?*
> A. I gained status in front of other kids when I didn't put up with it. They wished they could do the same but couldn't, so they looked up to me.

Like Hugh, Perry eventually defined his masculinity against the school and its overall project. He enjoyed a tough reputation and the masculine status it earned. Likewise he constructed an in-school exemplary masculinity.

At age fourteen and toward the end of his eighth-grade year, Perry was expelled from school (never to return); immediately after the expulsion his uncle died. The following is an extended dialogue of how this event—in conjunction with other circumstances—was a major turning point in Perry's life.

> When my uncle died I lost it for a long time. I didn't want to come out of my room. I just kinda wanted to be by myself. I couldn't get it through my head that he was dead and I couldn't picture him not being there for me—to be able to talk to, to be able to have him pick me up and do things with.
>
> Q. *Did your mother comfort you?*
> A. A little. But she was on my stepfather's side 'cause I got expelled. So she just gave up on me and defended my stepfather all the time.

Q. How did your stepfather respond to the death of your uncle?

A. He said he was sorry that my uncle died "but you've got chores to do." It was like that. I hated him for that, and so I ran away.

Q. You ran away from home?

A. Why stay? My uncle was dead. My mom sided with my stepfather. I hated my stepfather. And I was kicked out of school. I hated what was going on around me, so I just left and I'm glad I did.

Q. Where did you go when you ran away?

A. I went and stayed with friends at their house. Their parents would let me stay.

Q. Did you go to school?

A. No. I was expelled and they wouldn't let me back in. If my friends decided to go to school, I'd just hang out on the streets. I'd go and find ways to make money—like break into cars, break into stores, and people's houses.

Q. Why did you do that?

A. I needed some money, plus it was an adrenaline rush. Breaking into houses really got my adrenaline pumping, and then to run from the house and not get caught. It was fun 'cause I always got some cash and I always felt good about myself while I was doing it.

Q. Why did that feel good?

A. 'Cause I got away for it, and the people I lived with did it and we all laughed about how easy it was. We didn't have to work for a thing.

Q. Did you always do that alone?

A. At first alone but then a lot of my friends started dropping out and we would all hang together, get money to get drugs, get fried, and get some food.

Q. What kind of crimes did you commit?

A. Mostly breaking into cars and houses, and stealing cars. We would take all we could get our hands on. Houses was the most fun 'cause, you know, it was exciting to be in someone's house and go through all their shit. If we happened to be doing drugs at the time we broke into a house, we'd had the munchies and we'd go right for the refrigerator and help ourselves. At the time we really weren't worried about getting caught by the police, because we had like a flawless record, you know. We'd break into houses and we'd never get in trouble for it. We figured, hey, break into a house, get something to eat, take anything we'd want, and get out.

After being expelled from school, only three things were important to Perry and his friends: "getting laid, getting hammered, and getting fried. It all had to do with drugs, alcohol, and sex. It was just those three things." They sold what they stole to a local fence, using the money to rent an apartment, buy food, clothes, drugs, and alcohol.

Indeed, feeling disconnected to home and school, Perry was attracted to the "street life" because he was "getting something from the drugs and the alcohol and the sex that [he] wasn't getting from school and books, and that was a feeling inside." I asked Perry to describe that feeling for me:

It was the "rush," the freedom to do what I wanted to do with my friends. I didn't have my stepfather telling me what to do and teachers or principals telling me what to do, and I had people who cared for me. Like I said, we was like a family.

Perry did not characterize the people he hung out with as a "gang"[1] but rather as "just a group of friends who liked to hang out. We just kinda stuck together and just did things." There were no special "uniforms" or requirements to join this group:

The only thing you had to be in our group of friends was that you had to be there for each other. If someone needed back in a fight and someone needed some help with money or something like that, you'd be there to help them out. You didn't have to get beaten up by all of these people to get in our group of people. You didn't have to go do something to get in with our group of people. You just had to be a good guy, you know—a friend.

Q. Were there girls in your group?

A. Yeah. Some.

Q. Did they participate in the same crimes as the boys?

A. Yeah, sometimes. There was some girls that stole from stores and stuff. But mostly they just hang out and get hammered, get fried, and have sex with us.

Q. Was sex important to everyone in the group?

A. Oh yeah. We had like a competition. We would see how many girls we could screw in one week and how many nuts [orgasms] we could bust in one day.

Q. Is it ever appropriate to have sex with a girl if she does not want to?

A. Of course not. I heard of guys raping girls—but not my friends. We didn't need to 'cause the girls that hung out always wanted it, you know. That's what they lived for, you know.

Q. Were there "boyfriends" and "girlfriends" in your group?

A. No. We was just one happy family and we always meeting new girls, you know.

Q. What about homosexuality?

A. We didn't approve of it. As a matter of fact, we beat homosexuals up.

Q. Give me an example of that.

A. A bunch of them was having this big barbecue. And we went down there. We had already been drinking. We had a big van full of people, and my friend said, "Oh, look at all the faggots down there." And we all thought that was pretty funny, and then my friend said: "Let's go down there and beat some ass, go beat them faggots." And I was like "alright." So there were six or seven of us in the van, so we all went down and just started making fun of them. And one of the faggots told us to get the fuck away from them, and I went up to him and said, "Oh, you talking shit. You don't tell me to get the fuck out of here." And then I beat the shit out of him. It was fun until the cops came and we got arrested.

Q. Why did you assault that person?

A. 'Cause he was talking shit, and nobody talks shit to me.

Q. Do you engage in violence whenever someone "talks shit" to you?

A. When someone challenges me. When someone tries to intimidate me. When they get up in my face or if they hint that they want to fight me. If they get physical with me, I'm gonna get physical back.

Q. Did girls in your group fight?

A. No, they never did. That's one of the ways we see as being masculine. Girls are not aggressive and don't fight.

Q. What did you see as masculine when you were in the eighth grade?

A. Being tough, being good at sports, and having lots of people respect you.

Q. How about after being expelled from school?

A. Having courage to do things—like who had the biggest balls, who had the most courage. If you had balls enough to go and break into a house or steal a car, then you were something else. And being masculine was screwing the most girls, who could fight the best, who had the courage to do certain things, like I said, who could hold the most beer, smoke the most weed.

Like Hugh, Perry learned at home and at school that physical violence was an appropriate response to masculine threat. Indeed, such conduct defined the character of his mentor, subsequently of his masculinity, and Perry constructed practices at school and on the street that reproduced that masculinity. Perry used his physicality—and its accompanying masculine self-esteem—to dominate others in school and on the street. Predictably, Perry responded with assaultive violence when others challenged his masculinity.

Lenny

Lenny was a short, obese, and somewhat shy fifteen-year-old. Although he wore a cap to both interviews that was emblazoned "Give Blood, Play Hockey," he spoke to me in a skittish and soft-spoken manner.

Lenny lived in a working-class neighborhood with his mother, father, an older brother (age 18), and a younger sister (age 13). The family inhabited a two-bedroom upstairs apartment. Lenny had another brother (age 21) who did not live with the family. Lenny's earliest family memory is of the first time the family went camping: "We had a great time together, right by a lake, canoeing, hiking, roasting marshmallows, and stuff."

Although both parents worked outside the home in the unskilled labor market, the mother was responsible for all the domestic labor (the father did no domestic labor), receiving only limited help from the children. Lenny and his brother shared a room, and all three children were responsible for keeping their respective rooms clean. This was not a problem because Lenny and his brother alternated cleaning the room they shared, and there seemed to be little quarrel regarding this. Lenny also reported a very warm and affectionate family environment: "My parents have a kinda family thing. We do things together. We go to beaches, camping, have cookouts, go to the movies. A lot of things I guess." However, Lenny mostly liked to do things with his father. Asked about his favorite activities, Lenny replied,

> We go hunting each year. My father, my brothers, and me. My father bought me a 30/30. And I got my hunting license. My father helped me study to get my license. I studied with him. That was fun.

Asked further about hunting, Lenny said, "It's exciting to get ready 'cause we eat a big supper before and get up early and go. Its fun to be with my dad." I inquired about other activities Lenny did with his father and he emphasized "fishing, swimming, catch, play darts. The whole family, we play board games; that's real fun."

Lenny's mother never disciplined Lenny and the other children—it was the father who "took control" when he came home from work: "He never actually hit me, he just would get mad and talk serious to me. We didn't make him mad that much. We'd do what my dad and mom says."

Like the other boys in this study, Lenny grew up under a conventional gender division of labor. Both parents performed the "appropriate" gendered labor in the home. Although the father was never physically violent, clearly he had the power in the family and used that power to control all the decisions. For example, even when Lenny wanted to do something outside the home (e.g., go bike riding), he was not allowed to do it unless his father approved ahead of time. Lenny identified with his father, who was his initial model for developing a conception of masculinity. Lenny thrived on his father's approval, such as when he went hunting and when he shot his first deer ("Dad said he was real proud of me") and conceptualized maleness as in part entailing "working hard, being strong, a good hunter, and being like Dad."

Lenny did quite well in elementary and junior high school. For the most part he liked his teachers and the schools, and he earned average grades. Most recently, in eighth grade, he graduated with honors and for that he got a new bike: "All my uncles and aunts, my mom and dad, they all pitched in and bought me a eighteen-speed. Pretty cool."

Nevertheless, at school Lenny received constant verbal abuse because of his physical size and shape (shorter and heavier than the other boys and girls). Other children call him "a slob," a "fat pig," and a "punk." Moreover, at school kids continually abused him about his mother, whom they saw as extremely obese: "Kids always say my mom is so fat, you know, and things like that. Kids say that my mom is so stupid. They call her all kinds of names, and some swear words—like she has a elephant ass." Because of this peer abuse, Lenny developed a dislike of school: "I hated to go to school." When asked if he discussed this abuse with his mother and father, Lenny replied:

> My dad said that if somebody punches me, then I get the right to punch him back. If I'm being teased, I tease him right back. Call him names back. If they teasing me always, then my dad tells me that I should punch 'em back.

Lenny felt embarrassed at school because of his physical size and shape, and because of his obese mother. Moreover, because he was smaller than the kids abusing him, he felt insecure about responding as his father taught him. He stated that the people abusing him were the "tough guys" in the school:

> They was the popular tough guys, and everyone laughed when I didn't do nothin'. I couldn't. I felt really small in front of everybody.

Consequently, Lenny became a loner and attempted to avoid the "tough guys."

In addition, Lenny observed that other kids in school were being abused and that some of these kids "would do nothin', like me, and some would fight." It seems there were many fights in Lenny's school based on verbal abuse. Lenny recalled the following example: "One time I was sitting down by my locker and the big guys teased this kid. He [the abused boy] hit the kid back, and he [the big guy] had a lot of friends and they all jumped in on that one kid." Consequently, these types of events led Lenny to become frightened of interaction at school, and he attempted to avoid school as much as possible. Indeed, there were fights in Lenny's school "about once every month"; apparently kids would fight about "everything." Lenny provided another example:

> Like one time a kid stole the other kid's comic cards. When he was in the hallway with them, the other kid came over and the kid gave 'em back but he beat him up 'cause he took 'em, over that. The kid gave 'em back to him, but he still beat him up. So I was always scared to talk to kids. I'd never know what might happen. So I went to school, went to my classes, and then ran home.
>
> Q. *Are these tough kids looked up to in your school?*
> A. Oh yeah. They are the neat kids. Everybody wanted to be tough like them.
> Q. *You wanted to be tough like them too?*
> A. Yeah, I wanted to be like them.

Lenny wanted to be like the "tough guys" at school; he longed to go home and tell his father that he did not let anyone push him around at school. He was unable to be masculine as interaction with his father and at school had taught him, which terrified him: "I couldn't tell my dad that

I was afraid 'cause then even him, would call me a wimp, a scaredy-cat."
By the time Lenny was fourteen he lacked masculine resources and thus
felt extremely subordinate at school. Nevertheless, one event at school
provided the opportunity for Lenny to be as masculine as the other boys:

> Q. *Tell me about that.*
> A. There was this nerd of a kid that even I made fun of. He would
> wear high-waters.
> Q. *What are high-waters?*
> A. Kids that wear high pants.
> Q. *Okay, go on.*
> A. This high-water is real skinny and ugly. I'm bigger than him. So I
> go: "You look funny in those pants," and stuff like that. I called him a
> "nerd" and he said the same back to me. There was all these kids around,
> and so I beat him up in the hallway 'cause he called me a "nerd" and
> nobody liked him.
> Q. *Why did you hit him?*
> A. 'Cause he called me a name that I didn't like and I wasn't afraid of
> him.
> Q. *What did other kids say who saw you beat him up?*
> A. Some kids was happy 'cause nobody likes him. But some said I
> should pick on kids my own size. Plus I got ISS [in-school suspension].
> Q. *Did you tell your dad about this fight?*
> A. Yeah. I ran home and told him that this kid was making fun of me,
> so I beat him up and got ISS for it.
> Q. *Did your father talk to the school officials about the fight?*
> A. Nope. He was just happy I beat up the kid.
> Q. *Is that the only fight in school?*
> A. Yeah, 'cause he is the kid I can beat up at school. I can beat up kids
> in my neighborhood.

Lenny also provided detailed information about his involvement in
neighborhood violence. According to Lenny, numerous neighborhood
boys would constantly challenge him to physical fights. However, he developed specific criteria for his participation in such challenges:

> I fight if I can beat the kid. I got this kid next door, he calls me a "fag." I
> mean, there is no reason why he calls me a "fag" and my father said next

time he does that "beat him up." My father says if I don't fight him, he'll [father] fight me. So I beat the kid up and my father was happy.

Q. Was this kid smaller than you?

A. Oh yeah; I only fight kids I can beat up. My father says that's smart, you should only "pick the battles you can win."

Q. How did it make you feel when you beat up neighborhood kids?

A. It made me feel real good inside. I knew I wasn't a wimp anymore.

Q. Did it bother you that the boys you beat up were smaller than you?

A. No, 'cause of what my dad said, and I fought kids that called me names or said stuff about Mom.

Q. Who are your friends?

A. I don't have friends at school. Only kids in my neighborhood. I play with kids that are younger than me. We have fun together.

I discussed sexuality with Lenny. He told me he did not learn about sex from his parents but from "sex ed" class at school. He also heard kids talking about sex with each other at school: "Some kids, even fourteen- and fifteen-year-olds, you know, are having sex in my school. And they talk about it, right out loud." Lenny never had a girlfriend or went on a date. However, he occasionally attended school dances and danced with several girls, but nothing ever developed. After the dance "I'd just go home." He asked girls for dates numerous times, but all refused. This bothered him somewhat because he wanted a girlfriend with whom to experience sexuality. He also wanted to have someone close with whom he could talk.

Q. Did you ever feel you should have sex with girls?

A. No.

Q. Other kids were bragging about having sex and did that make you feel you should also have sex to be cool?

A. No, never. You don't have to have sex to be cool.

Lenny perceived himself as heterosexual without feeling that he had to "go out there and do it." If he had a girlfriend, he would like to experience sexuality because he was still a "virgin." However, Lenny pointed out that it did not bother him that he had not experienced sex: "It'll come someday." Although the "cool guys" were also the boys who publicly bragged about "getting laid," Lenny felt there existed numerous avenues to "being cool": "Some kids are cool because of the clothes they're wearing. Some kids smoke; some are tough; some play sports, roller blading, biking. Not all cool kids have sex."

Lenny added that there were four major boy cliques in his school—the "jocks" (the tough and cool guys), the "nerds," the "smart kids," and the "losers." He belonged to none of these groups and felt that some of the jocks most likely considered him a "nerd" and a "wimp" because they always abused him, not only for his size and shape but also because he did not "fight back" and did not participate in any sport: "The jocks always teased the nerds and make fun of them for not playing sports." According to the jocks, those (including Lenny) who did not play sports, especially football, and could not retaliate in kind when bullied were "wimps" and "nerds." In fact, Lenny stated that jocks often called him a "wimp" because he did not play football and because he was not tough: "The jocks called me a wimp because they said I was afraid of gettin' tackled and afraid of fighting."

Q. *Did you feel you were a "wimp" and a "nerd"?*

A. Yeah, I did. I wanted to be tough like them, and I was tough to some kids.

Q. *How did it make you feel when you were tough with some kids?*

A. I didn't feel like I was a wimp anymore. I felt good. My dad said there's always someone bigger. And that goes for the big kids too. There are people who can beat them up.

Q. *What does it mean, then, to be a "real man"?*

A. To be tough, have muscles. Just big like my father, he's about six feet something. A good fighter like the guys at school.

Q. *Do you want to be a "real man"?*

A. Yeah! I want to get muscles because I want to be kinda strong in case people fight me. I want to be able to get them down, not to hurt them, but to get them down so they don't hurt me. I don't want them to fight me. I want to be strong enough to get them down.

I asked Lenny if there was anything else that he would include in his definition of a "real man." Surprisingly, he stated the following: "A real man is also a gentleman. That's a man. A man that don't hit girls. A man that hits girls is not a man."

Q. *Where did you learn that?*

A. From my father. My sister used to hit me and I got really mad at her. I'd say, "I'm gonna punch you if you don't stop it." And my father says, "I don't think so." I threaten to punch her but my father says, "I don't think so."

Q. Your father taught you not to hit girls?

A. Yeah. He says boys should never hit girls. Its okay to hit boys but not girls. That's what he taught me.

Q. Did your father ever hit your mother?

A. Never.

When I asked Lenny whether there were gay and lesbian kids in his school, he stated that he did not know of any but that "there is a gay person in my family. My brother, he's gay." Lenny's older brother (the 21-year-old) is gay and his brother's sexual orientation seemed to be accepted by Lenny's family: "Yeah, my family don't care. He comes over to my house. My family likes him. We had a cookout with him and his boyfriend. We all had a great time."

Q. So you know the difference between heterosexuality and homosexuality?

A. Of course.

Q. Should you be heterosexual to be a "real man"?

A. What? My brother is a real man. He's tall like my father and he lifts weights in his basement, so he's strong. He bikes and jogs and stuff. And he could fight if he wanted.

Unlike Hugh and Perry, Lenny grew up in a nonviolent household that emphasized family cooperation and stability as well as sexual diversity and being a "gentleman" toward women. Nevertheless, his father, like Hugh's Gramps and Perry's stepfather, emphasized male power in the house and "fighting back" against other males as masculine criteria. Lenny wanted to satisfy his father's criteria as well as be like the tough guys at school. Consequently, Lenny felt comfortable verbally abusing a "high-water." When that boy retaliated verbally, Lenny understood that he was then permitted to publicly assault him at school. Moreover, he willingly fought smaller and younger neighborhood boys if they abused him as well. Thus Lenny practiced masculine power over a few neighborhood boys through assaultive violence. This in turn gave him a sense of masculine self-esteem because of the favorable appraisal he received from some of his peers and from his father for the physical violence.

Conclusion

The assaultive offender life histories show contrasting relationships between each boy and his parent or guardian: Lenny experienced a nonviolent and close relationship with both parents; Hugh suffered verbal and physical violence (the "switch") from Gramps but a warm relationship with Gram; Perry endured physical violence from his stepfather and neglect from his mother but enjoyed a close relationship with his uncle. Although all three had an interest in sports, Hugh participated in cooking and cleaning the gang's apartment and Lenny considered "a man that hits girls . . . not a man." Nevertheless, like Sam, John, and Zack, what all three boys experienced in common at home and at school was that each appropriated a definition of masculinity that emphasized the importance of male power, control of others, and the ultimate use of physical violence to solve interpersonal problems.

At school Hugh and Perry constructed a physical presence that was revered by their classmates. When their masculinity was challenged, they would not physically back down to anyone, including teachers and older and sometimes bigger boys. Both Hugh and Perry constructed themselves as "cool guys" who were "superior" to the "wimps" and were not afraid to physically challenge the teacher's authority. Indeed, their ability to act out in class, abuse those "subordinate" to them, and physically fight when provoked convinced Hugh and Perry of their own eminent masculine self-worth.

Lenny had a different experience at school. He was often abused for his physical size and shape and for not being "a man." Although Lenny accepted the notion that being masculine meant responding to provocation with physical violence, because he was physically small and obese in relation to the bullies, he was unable to respond in such a "manly" fashion. However, his abusive interaction with a physically smaller boy at school (the "high-water") and with several boys in his neighborhood allowed him the "right" to engage in assaultive violence. It was Lenny himself who helped construct the settings, the victims, and the forms of assaultive violence that authorized him to become a "real man." Lenny's assaultive violence against weaker and smaller boys became a contextual resource for accomplishing masculinity according to the situationally defined criteria at school and at home.

In the next chapter we will compare the sex offenders with the assaultive offenders and then go on to consider the nonviolent boys in Chapter 5.

NOTES

1. Although Perry characterizes his group of friends as *not* a "gang," his description of the "group" corresponds to recent definitions of "gang." For example, in a review of the literature on definitional issues, Decker and Van Winkle (1998, 31) argue that "a gang is an age-graded peer group that exhibits some permanence, engages in criminal activity, and has some symbolic representation of membership." Members of Perry's "group" did not get "jumped in" nor did they wear special "colors." Nevertheless, there was stability to the group, members frequently engaged in crime, and membership was symbolized by the physically violent protection of other group members.

4

From Predisposition
to Violent Event

Contemporary theoretical arguments in criminology contend that crime can be understood only through conceptualization of "predisposition" and "criminal event" (Clarke and Cornish 1985; Gottfredson and Hirschi 1990; Tittle 1995). "Predisposition" generally refers to differences among individuals in their propensity to commit crime; "criminal event" refers to the criminal acts themselves. The life histories reported in Chapters 2 and 3 show that any explanation of varieties of violence committed by working-class adolescent males must take into account both predisposition to engage in violence and social situational factors, such as criminal motivations and opportunities. However, as stated in Chapter 1, the term "predisposition" is utilized here *not* as a stable trait developed early in life and continuing throughout the life course relatively unchanged. Rather, predisposition refers to the appropriation of a particular masculine resource in a specific milieu that constructs a tendency or an inclination to act in distinct ways during certain forms of social interaction. For the six violent boys in this study, "fighting back" was emphasized as a masculine resource in the reciprocal social settings of home and school, and each boy appropriated it as fitting conduct within that milieu. Indeed, it was a culturally prescribed "strategy of action" (Swidler 1986) that encouraged a specific line of gendered action. Logically, then, Chapter 4 examines—through the lens of structured action theory—the relationship among predisposition, masculinity challenges, motivation, opportunity, and differing forms of violence in the six case studies presented in Chapters 2 and 3. Chapter 5 summarizes the nonviolent boys' life histories. Chapter 6 compares the violent and nonviolent life histories and proposes social policies for curbing adolescent male violence.

Family, School, and
Violent Predispositions

Contemporary criminological work argues that the family is strongly and directly related to youth crime. In particular, such "family process variables" as lack of parental attachment, supervision, and discipline are said to be the most "important family correlates of serious, persistent delinquency" (Sampson and Laub 1993, 96). Indeed, most criminological discussions of the relationship between the family and youth crime emphasize parental *control* of adolescent behavior. For example, a recent review of the literature reveals that one of the best predictors of youth crime is whether or not parents supervise their children (LaFree 1998). Additionally, Gottfredson and Hirschi (1990) argue that low self-control is established in early childhood by parents who do not closely monitor the child's behavior, do not recognize deviant behavior when it occurs, and do not punish such behavior. Moreover, Hirschi (1995, 128) has most recently argued that attachment to parents "facilitates supervision and discipline" and deters delinquency "independent of its indirect effects on socialization and self-control."

However, in these accounts of family process variables the parent–child interaction is assumed to be unidirectional, that is, youth are either controlled by parents or they are not, and thus youth display little if any creativity; their actions, including crime, are simply the result of parental action. Parents, it seems, are the sole actors in the family interactional drama. This line of thought, of course, ignores the fact that youth are active agents in their familial social relations and fails to account for the intentions of youth and how youthful social action is a meaningful construction in itself.

In addition, the three sex offenders and three assaultive offenders *varied* regarding family process variables. For example, two of the boys (Sam and Lenny) were very attached to both of their parents and engaged in considerable and warm interaction with them. Moreover, these boys were supervised and disciplined consistently by their parents. From these two boys' point of view, the parents were able to perceive misbehavior, and the boys were controlled effectively when it occurred. Arguably, the cases of Sam and Lenny directly challenge control theories, indicating that other variables may be more important for eventual engagement in violence than control theorists acknowledge.

Nevertheless, two sex offenders (John and Zack) and two assaultive offenders (Hugh and Perry) experienced significantly violent and oppressive interactions with parents or guardians, although in different ways. In review, John suffered verbal, physical, and sexual violence at the hands of his stepfather and had an unreliable mother; Zack experienced physical and verbal violence from his aunt but had a warm relationship with his uncle and grandmother; Hugh was exposed to verbal and physical violence from Gramps but enjoyed a warm relationship with Gram; and Perry experienced verbal and physical violence from his stepfather and neglect from his mother but had a close relationship with his uncle. Compared with Sam and Lenny, these four boys lacked effective parental supervision and experienced traumatic and emotionally difficult events in the family. All four boys had different experiences within the family, especially regarding relationships with the most influential adults in their lives. And with the exception of John, each boy had a close and warm interaction with—indeed was attached to—at least one nonviolent adult.

Consequently, the six life histories suggest a much more complex familial interaction than control theories contemplate. Although the family is a significant setting for the initial formation of self and, simultaneously, an important dimension for understanding the initial processes by which "innocent tots" are transformed into "violent teenagers," we must go beyond the narrow focus on parental control and attachment and examine how family interaction and practices help us understand—through its reciprocal connection to the school—the social construction of violent predispositions. Indeed, attachment is rarely defined in the criminological literature—especially what can be learned through that attachment or lack of it. This is important because it was not a lack of control or attachment or an experience of traumatic and emotionally difficult family events that defined the similarity among all six families. Rather, it was the appropriation of physically violent predispositions by each boy as a crucial characteristic of what it means to be a "real man."

Moreover, control theories dismiss the interplay between home and school. Indeed, violent predispositions are not simply appropriated in the family. Rather, as shown in the lives of these six boys, they attempted to resolve oppressive situations at school in ways related to their interactions at home with adults as well as through their interactions at school. Thus it is the interrelatedness of home and school, and the choices made

by each boy during that interchange, that resulted in the social construction of violent predispositions. Let's examine this more systematically.

Engagement with Hegemonic Masculinity

All the families in this study were working class and lived in the center of
a New England city (or working-class suburb), and all six violent boys
subsequently attended working-class schools. The majority of families
lived in rented houses, apartments, or trailers. Life was economically
stressful, the families living from paycheck to paycheck, even though
usually both parents worked in the wage-labor market.

Within the six working-class families, three patterns of male attachment emerged: Sam and Lenny identified strongly with their nonviolent
father; Hugh and John were influenced by a violent grandfather and stepfather, respectively; and Perry and Zack bonded closely to a benevolent
uncle. The boys' lives involved a variety of adult-male role models; nevertheless, the single most important principle communicated to each boy
by each of these adult males was the notion of hegemonic masculinity. In
particular, the life history data show that all six boys grew up in an environment that articulated for them a *practiced* definition of masculine
power. In the majority of these families, the boys found themselves in
gender inegalitarian milieus in which adult women were expected to do
the bulk of domestic labor (while also working outside the home) and
adult men were expected to exercise power over women and children. Indeed, the gender division of labor (except in Zack's family) embraced
adult male power to define the household setting only in adult male
terms and imprinted on each boy that women are here to serve men. Even
in families in which both parents worked outside the home, male power
was deemed an authentic and acceptable part of familial social relations.
This legitimized power provided these adult men with considerably
greater authority in the family. Consequently, through interactions in the
family the boys acquired a definition of masculinity that was constructed
in opposition to, and with control over, women.

Although children become aware of their "sex category" at an early age
(West and Zimmerman 1987), gender construction is an ongoing project
that involves interaction and negotiation within specific social settings.
The family, of course, is one such social setting and family interaction is a
significant resource that boys draw upon for learning about masculinity.
All the violent boys (albeit in different ways) were attached to an adult

male in the family: father, stepfather, grandfather, or uncle. In addition to learning that men exercise control over women—and regardless of whether they grew up in violent or nonviolent homes—this "attachment" reproduced other specific notions of masculinity. For example, Sam wanted to be a mechanic like his dad, Zack's uncle instilled in him a liking for sports, and Lenny's dad taught him to be a hunter. These types of interaction are not unusual in working-class families (e.g., successfully performing masculine practices for Dad) and are key to developing emotional attachments to influential adult men in the formative years of many working-class boys (Messner 1992). By reason of these interactions with adult males, then, each of the six boys undertook to practice what was being preached and represented. Connell (1995, 122) defines this proactive adoption of "family values" (such as manual and athletic skills and male power and control over others) as the "moment of engagement" with hegemonic masculinity, "the moment at which the boy takes up the project of hegemonic masculinity as his own." Although constructed in different ways, such moments of engagement occurred in each of these lives through interactions—moments when the boys alone helped engineer their newly professed masculinities.

Nevertheless, engagement with hegemonic masculinity is not a group of isolated events found solely in the family. As noted earlier, as boys work their way through school, their notions of what it means to be "a man" are likewise formed through interactions at school. Indeed, boys construct masculinities through the continual interchanges between home and school.

Constructing Violent Predispositions

For all the sex offenders and assaultive offenders an important part of engagement with hegemonic masculinity entailed a predisposition to *physical* violence. This is not surprising inasmuch as in industrialized societies hegemonic masculinity is strongly associated with aggressiveness and capacity for violence (Connell 1995). Particularly in U.S. society—with one of the highest rates of interpersonal violence of the industrialized countries—there remains a strong cultural connection between admired masculinity and violent response to threat. Indeed, man/boy aggression and capacity for violence are distinct characteristics of U.S. hegemonic masculinity. Reflecting those characteristics conveys not simply material rewards but admiration, esteem, and social power as well (Kaufman 1998).

Male violence is not merely culturally glorified, as Anne Campbell (1993, 31) rightly argues, it is "so tightly tied to masculinity" that "aggression becomes central to the boy's notion of manhood." As Campbell (pp. 35–36) continues:

> The men who employ aggression are heroes: the president whose army returns in triumph from a foreign war; the subway rider who shoots his assailants and instantaneously shifts from victim to victor; the movie star whose trademark is an icy stare and the wordless and cold-blooded use of lethal violence. The boy sees that the successful use of force not only gains territory or toys, it brings with it admiration and esteem.

Yet the culture does more than this; it simultaneously defines when and how to use violence, that is, at what time aggression is appropriate and is the proper means of violence to employ. As Kaufman (1998, 5) shows, masculine violence "has long been institutionalized as an acceptable means of solving conflicts." More specifically, male involvement in physical violence is legitimate as long as it occurs within the context of standing up to threat. To question or to criticize male behavior is to assert male social inferiority and to deny respect; without respect there can be no masculine self-esteem (Campbell 1993). The proper cultural and therefore hegemonic masculine response is some type of physical return in kind. To back off minimizes risk of physical injury but maximizes loss of face and consequently reduces masculine power (Campbell 1993; Kaufman 1998).

This hegemonic masculine notion of the proper response to threat is especially emphasized in working-class communities. For example, Heimer's (1997) recent review of the criminological literature on youth violence and social class showed that both aggregate-level research and self-report studies consistently report that the highest rates of violent crime occur among working-class males. Moreover, Luckenbill and Doyle (1989, 431) reported that among teenage working-class males in particular, "disputatiousness and aggressiveness are most pronounced when a negative outcome involves an equal's attack on the self in a public setting." Working-class communities are more likely than middle- and upper-class communities to sanction male physical violence as an appropriate response when characteristics of the self are attacked. All communities construct "regulative rules"—social rules that define the appropriate response to threat. Particularly for working-class communities, physical violence is frequently the preferred response (Bernard 1990, 62).

Neal Shover (1996, 91) reviewed the literature on working-class masculine identity and concluded that throughout much of the working class masculinity is equated with toughness and courage:

> These men are judged by how they respond to challenges of one kind or another. The ability to take care of oneself in a world where challenge and adversity are thought to be inevitable counts as a prime virtue. . . . when one is insulted or "disrespected," a violent response is condoned if not expected.

Finally, Heimer's (1997) study supports Shover's conclusion by showing that working-class youth are more likely than middle-class youth to engage in violent crime because they have learned definitions supportive of violence through interaction with their parents and peers. Primarily through parenting practices and interaction with aggressive peers, working-class youth learn that "coercion and force can be used to resolve problems" (p. 807).

Thus it comes as no surprise that *all* the sex and assaultive offenders in this study actively appropriated this conception of masculinity at home and at school. All the violent offenders were committed to the belief that the use of physical violence is an appropriate means to solve interpersonal problems. Regardless of whether they grew up in violent or nonviolent homes, or who the males were to whom they were attached (father, stepfather, grandfather, uncle), they learned that physical violence is the fitting and well-chosen masculine response to threat—a "real man" was obligated to respond in this fashion. In short, the life histories show how each offender, in interaction within the family (but especially with a specific adult male) and at school, actively participated in the social construction of physically violent and controlling predispositions.

The six violent offender life stories validate Heimer's (1997) conclusion that parents and youths are active agents in the construction of definitions supportive of violence. At the same time, the life stories add to Heimer's conclusion in three significant ways. First, predispositions to violence are actively appropriated and grasped by boys not simply through interaction with parents but through *gendered* interaction and as *participants* in the ongoing, collective family definitions of appropriate masculine practices. Indeed, the data offer insight into how physical violence as a means to solve problems is routinely reproduced in certain families and, as such, provides boys with a meaningful way to construct masculinity and become attached to an adult male. Second, Heimer (p. 807) emphasizes learning definitions supportive of violence through interaction with parents who engage in "power-assertive discipline" such as verbal commands and physical punishment. Although these disciplines occurred in most of the violent boys' families, this clearly was not the case in all six families. Indeed, some of the working-class families (e.g., Sam's and Lenny's) emphasized nonassertive disciplinary practices. What unites all six families in this study is not power-assertive discipline but a family conception of what it means to be a "real man." For each family that conception was clearly demonstrated by the belief that it is legitimate masculine behavior to respond to threat with physical violence, which is *the* appropriate means of solving problems. Third, a predisposition to violence was likewise appropriated at school, where all six boys found themselves as either victims or perpetrators of peer abuse—what Kindlon and Thompson (1999, 72–93) call the "culture of cruelty." Within the peer culture of all schools, boys face verbal abuse for any failure to conform: "*Anything* a boy says or does that's different can and will be used against him" (p. 73). In other words, the culture of cruelty is an interactional environment in which "a boy is tutored away from trust, empathy, and relationship" and participates instead in a

> world of developing masculinity in which everything he does or thinks is judged on the basis of the strength or weakness it represents: you are either strong and worthwhile, or weak and worthless. He must also be willing to fight. Even if you have never fought, and never intend to fight, you have to pretend to yourself that you can and will. A respected boy is someone who can "handle himself." (pp. 75, 79)

Thus the culture of cruelty constructs hierarchy among boys and demands, as does the broader working-class culture, that boys respond to such abuse through physical violence. Indeed, all six violent boys either participated in this culture as bullies (Hugh, Perry, and eventually Lenny) or as victims (Sam, John, Zack, and Lenny) but wanted to retaliate physically. Consequently, these boys derived a predisposition to violence not simply through interaction with parents but also in the *culture of schools*. For each boy the significant male adult(s) at home in turn buttressed that culture by encouraging them to "fight back" to provocation. Although Heimer's data shows that association with aggressive peers leads to learning violent definitions, she misses the interrelationship and mutually reinforcing interaction of home and school and the exact nature of the interaction among boys within the school milieu (see also Heimer and De Coster 1999).

In sum, what the violent boys' life stories reveal is reciprocal interaction of gender practices within the family and school. Sons trained to do manual "hands-on" work and/or engage in sport; boys who actively identified with and therefore attached to a powerful father and/or other adult male; boys who wanted to be like *him* and acted out what *he* preached and represented (such as "fighting back" to provocation at school)—these gender "family practices" arose from their collective class-structured situations in which each family member, in turn, contributed to the reproduction of class and gender social structures. Through their life histories, we have witnessed social actions by family members and their creative and active responses to situations presented to them by social structures. The result is engaging certain aspects of hegemonic masculinity and launching specific types of *working-class masculinity*.

Part of this working-class masculinity is a predisposition to violence. Each of the violent boys appropriated from both home and school (albeit in different ways) that when aspects of the self were attacked, the proper masculine response was to "fight back" physically. In other words, the boys actively accepted, through interaction at home and school, that the suitable and legitimate response to threat was physical retaliation—this social action was emphasized as a masculine resource. Thus the life histories show how eventual violent offenders, interacting in the family and at school, actively participated in the construction of a masculinity that included predispositions to violence and simultaneously reproduced class and gender social structures.

However, predisposition to violence does not in itself guarantee violence. For violence to emerge, those so predisposed must be motivated toward violence and once motivated must experience the opportunity to engage in violence. For the six violent boys, such motivation for violence developed in the social setting of school. The culture of cruelty in junior high and high school figured significantly in each boy's narrative as a major site for masculine confrontation. From substantially analogous working-class circumstances the six boys took different paths and committed different types of violence and victimization based in part on their position within their peer culture. The sex offenders became *solitary offenders* (they committed violence in private and were the lone offenders); they specialized in sexual violence (they never committed another type of crime); and they repeatedly victimized the same person (a much less powerful female and one male). Two of the assaultive offenders—Hugh and Perry—became *social offenders* (they committed crimes with accomplices and in public); they were versatile in their criminality (they engaged in a variety of crimes); and when they committed violence it was exclusively assaultive violence against both acquaintances and strangers. One of the assaultive offenders (Lenny) was also a *social offender* who committed his physical violence alone but in public and never engaged in any other type of crime; Lenny is an assaultive specialist. What is interesting about the six life stories is not the violence per se but the differing types of violence and contextual victimization. How did these differences evolve? Analyzing agency and its relation to the body in the context of school can help answer this question.

Schooling, the Body, and Motivation for Violence

School dynamics are key to understanding the different life courses taken by the sex offenders and the assaultive offenders—each dynamic focusing on the body and its relation to masculine construction.

Making Bodies Matter

Research shows that the tallest and strongest boys in junior high and high school are usually the most popular—admired by peers (and parents and teachers) for their size and athletic prowess (Thorne 1993). These are the masculine "cool guys" who participate in school athletics and who—usually on weekends—defy adult authority by "partying" (e.g., experimenting with drugs, alcohol, and sex) (Eckert 1989; Foley 1990; Lefkowitz 1997). In the context of school, a boy's height and musculature increase self-esteem and prestige and create a more positive body image (Thorne 1993). Research on male adolescent development shows that boys are acutely aware of their pubertal changing selves as well as other people's responses to those changes (Petersen 1988). Moreover, research on adolescents demonstrates that girls are more likely to *act on* their bodies whereas boys *act through* their bodies (Martin 1996). Boys who participate in sports, for example, state that "they take pleasure in their agency and their bodies simultaneously. They feel like they accomplish things in their bodies and in their lives" (p. 55). That is, they "feel" masculine through bodily performance. Thus puberty is associated with a higher degree of concern about bodily images and practices than are other age categories. A boy who does not have the appropriate body shape and size and is unable to use his body in a masculine way frequently experiences distress (Petersen 1988). In the "teen" world bodies are increasingly subject to inspection and surveillance by peers, and in the culture of cruelty physically small, less muscular, nonathletic boys are often labeled "wimps" and "fags" (Kindlon and Thompson 1999). In junior high and high school, masculine social hierarchies develop in relation to somatic type. Such somatic differentiation affirms inequality among boys, and diverse masculinities are thus constructed in relation to biological development (Canaan 1987; Connell 1995; Thorne 1993). The relationship among these masculinities forms a specific social structure within the social situation of the school. In short, today the body has become increasingly crucial to self-image, especially among teenage youth. Through interaction at school, adolescents "make bodies matter" by constructing some bodies as more masculine than others.

Historically, criminological interest in the male body has followed two paths. On the one hand, crime proceeds from certain *types of male bodies*; on the other hand, crime ultimately, but not exclusively, results from the *generic male body itself*. The former view is associated with biologically based multifactor theorists such as William Sheldon (1949) and Sheldon Glueck and Eleanor Glueck (1956), the latter being associated with certain "sex-role" theorists (see Messerschmidt 1993, 14–29). For example, Sheldon (1949) argued for the existence of three major male body types: endomorph (short, soft, and rounded body); mesomorph (lean and muscular body); and ectomorph (fragile and skinny body). Sheldon concluded that juvenile delinquents were significantly more mesomorphic and less ectomorphic than nondelinquents. Seven years later, in *Physique and Delinquency* (1956), Glueck and Glueck reported that mesomorphs made up about 60 percent of all delinquents and that the alleged mesomorphic body lent itself naturally to the commission of violent acts (p. 226). Consequently, Sheldon and the Gluecks centered their criminological inquiry in part on the *differences* among males in terms of body type in their search for *the* criminal man.

Edwin Sutherland established the sociological model of crime as the dominant paradigm in criminology by vehemently attacking, in particular, the Gluecks' multifactor approach (Laub and Sampdon 1991). As Laub and Sampson (p. 1404) conclude in their analysis of the famous Sutherland–Glueck debate:

[A] shift in Sutherland's disciplinary and methodological outlook resulted in a theory that virtually required him to destroy individual-level,
or nonsociological, perspectives on crime. The Gluecks advocated a
multi-factor theory of crime, which to Sutherland represented a threat to
the intellectual status of sociological criminology. Hence, Sutherland's
attack was aimed largely at extinguishing their interdisciplinary model
so that sociology could establish proprietary rights to criminology.

The rise of sociological criminology was sustained simultaneously by
additional research demonstrating that "physique does not cause crime,
nor is it an inevitable correlate of it" (Wilson and Herrnstein 1985, 89). As
a result of these developments, sociological criminology argued for a
strict dichotomy between "society" and "the body," focusing on the former as exclusively defining the realm of criminological inquiry. To avoid
any inclination to biological reductionism, sociologically oriented criminologists since Sutherland have treated each part of this dichotomy as un-
connected intellectual domains that necessitate separate analysis. Indeed,
in contemporary sociological criminology, the male body appears only in
discussions of "gender and crime" in which it is cryptically argued that
the body establishes *generic* differences between men and women, and society culturally elaborates the distinction through the socialization of
"gender roles" (see Messerschmidt 1993, 14–29). This "gender role theory" was adopted wholeheartedly by Sutherland and most criminologists
after him because it asserts that differences between the "generic male"
and the "generic female" are socially rather than biologically constructed.
Following Sutherland, criminologists have flaunted what Scott and Morgan (1993) call an "anti-body bias."
    Although work on the social construction of gender and crime proved
to be an important and essential development within sociological (and in
particular feminist) criminology, one disadvantage is that criminological
scholars have ignored how those who engage in crime interact with and
through their bodies. Since Sutherland's rise to prominence in criminology, the body has been completely untheorized by sociological criminologists; although the body is materially present yet theoretically absent, the
emphasis of criminological analysis is clearly on the social.
    Any consideration of the six violent boys' life stories necessitates
"bringing the body back in" to sociological criminology. The body must
be at the center, rather than the fringe, of our analysis because the data
clearly show that we must take into account the intent of these boys as so-

cial actors and how their social actions relate to the body as meaningful constructions in themselves. As Bryan Turner (1984, 112) argues in *The Body and Society*, the self can be understood only as constructed through the presentation of the body in everyday life: "Successful images require successful bodies, which have been trained, disciplined, and orchestrated to enhance our personal value." Connell (1995, 54–61) distinctively adds that an understanding of the body must focus on agency. He argues that bodies participate in social action by delineating courses of social conduct: Bodies are both objects and agents of social practice and, given the context, will do certain things and not others. Indeed, our bodies constrain or facilitate social action and therefore mediate and influence social practices. "The consequence of bodily practice is historicity: the creation and transformation of situations. Bodies are drawn into history and history is constituted through bodies" (Connell 1998, 7). In short, it is impossible to consider human agency—and, therefore, the differing forms of violence by the boys in this study—without taking the body into account. Their life histories clearly show the importance of the body to the definition of self and therefore to the choices made by all six violent boys.

All the sex offenders—and one of the assaultive offenders (Lenny)—saw themselves as physically "not measuring up" to the school view of the ideal masculine body. As a result of school interaction these boys were defined as constituting a subordinate body, which they eventually accepted and thereby demonstrated subordinate masculinity. These boys perceived themselves as not simply flunking the body test—they were not muscular or tall and could not play ball—but simultaneously as being publicly degraded for their physical size and shape. For these four boys, then, their bodies were a *restraint* on their agency—they could not do the masculine practices the "cool guys" were doing—and this somatic limitation was extremely troubling to them. In all four cases, lack of bodily performance, in particular their inability to "fight back" when bullied by the "tough guys," as well as their "inferior" body shapes and structures, convinced them that they were not only different from the "cool guys" at school but were also subordinate to them. In other words, their bodies did not live up to their contextual masculine expectations and consequently created an in-school masculinity challenge. Indeed, they were socially constructed in school as the "other."[1]

Two of the assaultive boys (Hugh and Perry), however, did physically "measure up." They participated in school sport and constructed a physical presence in school that was revered by their classmates. These assaultive offenders were tall and muscular for their age. When their masculinity was challenged on the playground or in the classroom, they would not physically back down to anyone, including teachers or older, sometimes bigger boys. For these two assaultive boys, their bodies *facilitated* masculine agency—they successfully constructed themselves as "cool guys" who were "superior" to many other boys. Indeed, their ability to act out in class, bully those "subordinate" to them, and physically fight when provoked convinced them of their own eminent masculine self-worth.

In short, what these six life stories reveal is that a boy's masculine school existence is in part dependent on *the capacity for power that he embodies.* As Chris Shilling (1993, 113) put it, "This power is always an active power, a power which can be exercised on and over others. If a man's physicality is unable to convey an image of power, he is found to have little presence precisely because the social definition of men as holders of power is not reflected in his embodiment."

To enjoy a sense of "presence" and masculine self-esteem, the male body must at the very least suggest the promise of forceful and vigorous physicality. In other words, the body intervenes in social interaction as a personal resource that socially symbolizes a boy's masculine identity and therefore represents a site of either power or powerlessness.

Making Sexualities Matter

The importance of corporeal differentiation notwithstanding, the school also organizes masculine difference and inequality through constructs of sexuality. Adolescence is a time in life when agency and body become connected to sexuality (Martin 1996). Studies of school and sexuality show that to "do" heterosexuality is an everyday dominant masculine bodily practice in junior high and high school and that such sexual orientation is an important source of acceptable male identity (Connell 1996; Mac an Ghaill 1994; Martin 1996). Particularly within male group "sex talk" at school, "sex" is not simply "being heterosexual"; one must not be homosexual (Holland, Romazanoglu, and Sharpe 1993; Thorne 1993; Wood 1984). Adolescent boys use sexuality to establish hierarchies by constructing practices that are heterosexual dominant–gay subordinate. As Kindlon and Thompson (1999, 81) point out, adolescent boys do not usually understand where homosexuality comes from, "but they do know it's not a 'cool' thing to be. Homosexuals are male, but they aren't *manly."* One of the ways, then, to validate masculinity at school is to express and define oneself as heterosexual both by degrading homosexuality and by engaging in heterosexual practices. Moreover, boys who show no interest in girls, who lack social skills to make heterosexual contact, who lack knowledge of the female body, and who do not degrade homosexuality are labeled "fags" and are therefore publicly represented as demonstrating subordinate sexuality and masculinity (Holland, Ramazanoglu, and Sharpe 1993). The relationships among sexualities form a social structure within the social setting of school. As Allan Hunter (1993, 153) pointed out, to be constructed as a "fag" is to be placed "on the inside of homophobia, surrounded by it, experiencing it constantly. You don't even have to be physically attracted to males to get in." In other words, the "heterosexual sissy" is, like the gay male, positioned inside homophobic oppression.

Indeed, at school the "cool guys" not only are tall, strong, and athletic but are actively and publicly involved in heterosexuality; announced genital potency is another form of in-school masculine bodily performance. Not surprisingly, in the social situation of the six violent boys' schools, the criteria of dominant masculinity included these bodily features. Consequently, like physicality, the construction of masculinity through heterosexual performance means that masculinity is especially challenged when such sexual performance cannot be realized. In her examination of adolescent agency, body, and sexuality Karin Martin (1996) found that teenage boys want to engage in heterosexuality because it reinforces masculine and adult status. Moreover, she discovered that once boys engage in heterosexuality, this makes them feel accomplished: "After sex, boys feel more agentic, masculine, adult, and bonded with other men. In particular, they feel like they are able to will something and make it happen, and to do so in the realm of sexuality" (p. 14). Boys who want to engage in heterosexuality but for whatever reason are unable to do so develop a negative masculine self-esteem. As Martin (p. 10) continues, for adolescent boys, engaging in sexuality "is necessary for a positive sense of self. . . . Sexual subjectivity is a necessary component of agency and thus of self-esteem." As the link between agency and body becomes connected to sexuality in adolescence, boys develop differing levels of self-esteem depending upon their ability to make that connection.

As with the body, contemporary criminology has ignored the importance of sexuality to one's sense of self. Although snippets exist in a few discussions of hate crimes, for the most part sexuality has historically been untheorized by criminologists. Like the body, sexuality is taken for granted, and the ways sexualities impact social action are disregarded. Yet the connection between sexuality and masculinity is undeniable. As Fracher and Kimmel (1998, 457) have shown, the foundation on which men construct sexuality is gender: "It is through our understanding of masculinity that we construct a sexuality, and it is through our sexuality that we confirm the successful construction of our gender identity. Gender informs sexuality; sexuality confirms gender." Past criminological research and theory neglect the relationship among masculinity, sexuality, and violence. The six violent boys' life stories once again demand that we consider the social construction of heterosexuality and the effects that sexuality has on individual practice, including sexual and assaultive violence.

The sex offenders observed the "cool guys" (and for Zack the "misfits" as well) at school sexualizing girls as objects of heterosexual desire and actually realizing such heterosexual expectations. Likewise, they objectified girls and wanted to participate in these same sexual practices themselves but were unable to achieve such masculine expectations. The sex offenders found their own sexuality through interaction with "the guys" at school and engaging in heterosexuality was for them an important resource for doing masculinity. Once again, however, their bodies restrained their agency, and their eventual subordination was intensely distressing to them. In short, the sex offenders were constructed in school as embodying a subordinate sexuality, which itself added another masculinity challenge.

The assaultive offenders had different school experiences. For both Hugh and Lenny sexuality was not an important issue, although for different reasons. For Hugh it was not necessary to be sexual publicly (until he joined the gang); participating in sports, acting out in class, bullying the "wimps," and fighting on the playground were more than adequate bodily resources with which to effectively accomplish masculinity in the context of school. Hugh's bodily performance in other masculine areas permitted him the "luxury" of disregarding, in the particular context of school, the sexual realm. Likewise, for Lenny it was not necessary to be sexual because, according to him, one can be "cool" in numerous ways. Lenny identified himself as heterosexual but accepted his brother as simultaneously gay *and* masculine, effectively diluting the connection of heterosexuality to masculinity. Finally, Perry's uncle defined sexuality for him as a relationship between men and women, and Perry's interaction at school reinforced this definition. Perry's peer group put pressure on him to "get laid" and his friend organized his first heterosexual experience when he was thirteen years old. After that he had no problem meeting girls and frequently engaged in sexual intercourse.

Although heterosexuality seemed to be a taken-for-granted part of growing up for Sam, Zack, Hugh, Perry, and Lenny, the case of John is different and particularly instructive. That heterosexuality is "normalized" in popular culture does not mean that it is necessarily realized in practice (Connell 1995). When John was being sexually victimized by his stepfather, he came to view the homosexual violence as "normal sexuality." It was not until he entered high school and came into contact with the sexual practices prevalent there that he became aware of the prohibition on homosexuality. Consequently, he developed guilt feelings for "being gay," and it was then that he decided to "become heterosexual." Thus same-sex contact in early childhood does not necessarily prevent the development of heterosexual practices. As Connell (1995, 149) has shown, "Young peoples' sexuality is a field of possibilities, not a deterministic system. . . . Sexuality is something that happens, that is produced by specific practices, not something predetermined. The sexual closure involves choice of an object."

Indeed, in all six life histories we can "see" object choice and an eventual sexual closure taking place in school. All six boys ultimately "became heterosexual," although differing in time and degree, and this consolidation of their sexuality clearly was related to in-school hegemonic masculinity. As "deviant" sexual identities were publicly ridiculed, policed, and repressed in school through the culture of cruelty, heterosexuality became for them a fundamental indication of "maleness." However, it was not simply heterosexuality, but a particular type of heterosexuality—in-school hegemonic masculinity centered on an alleged insatiable sexual appetite for women and on heterosexual performance as a hallmark of one's identity as a "cool guy." Girls and "wimps" were framed in school as the "other" against which "cool guys" constructed dominant masculinity.

The sex and assaultive offenders, then, shared with others at school specific social structural space and in the process participated in the construction of common blocks of knowledge in which masculine ideals and practices became institutionalized. The particular criteria of dominant masculine identities in school are embedded in the social situations and in the recurrent practices by which in-school social relations are structured (Giddens 1989). Nevertheless, differences among boys at school hinge in part on the body and sexuality and therefore on how they construct masculinity. Thus "cool guy" masculinity (Hugh and Perry) is sustained through its *bodily* and *sexual* relation to situationally defined "wimp" masculinity (Sam, John, Zack, and Lenny), even within the same class and school context. Boys in the same social class (and even in the same working-class school) are distinguished through different constructions of the body and sexuality and, therefore, masculinity. Consequently, constructs of "cool guy" and "wimp" inflect any class commonality with difference that produces power or powerlessness in relation to each other.

Violent Events

Clearly the *differing* masculinity challenges at school motivated these six boys toward differing forms of violence. As pointed out in Chapter 1, masculinity challenges are contextual interactions that result in masculine degradation. Masculinity challenges—such as the peer abuse suffered by Sam, John, Zack, and Lenny and the authoritarianism experienced by Hugh and Perry—arise from interactional threats and insults from peers, teachers, parents, and from unachievable situationally defined masculine expectations. Both, in various ways, proclaim a boy subordinate in contextually defined masculine terms. Because "doing gender" is an ongoing concern (West and Fenstermaker 1995), masculinity challenges arguably motivate social action toward masculine resources (e.g., "fighting back") that correct the subordinating social situation. Various forms of crime can be the result. Given that such interactions question, undermine, and/or threaten one's masculinity, only contextually "appropriate" masculine practices can help overcome the challenges.

Nevertheless, regardless of the quantity and quality of masculinity challenges, the choice of violence as an appropriate masculine response depends upon there being an opportunity for violence to occur. Social settings provide the resources and, therefore, opportunities for committing certain types of violence. Although the motivation to commit crime is activated by masculinity challenges, one must have the opportunity to engage in violence for violence to actually take place (e.g., access to a potential victim).

Doing Sexual Violence

Chapter 1 identified several weaknesses in previous research on adolescent male sexual violence, in particular, the scant use of comparison groups composed of boys from different family configurations and the failure to consider offender agency and gender. Although three case studies of sex offenders do not constitute a representative sample, they do suggest that important aspects of sexual violence committed by teenage males have been overlooked—especially the significance of certain bodily and heterosexual practices to adolescent masculine construction. The sexually violent victimization of John by his stepfather clearly directed John's victimization of the seven-year-old boy. Yet that specific sexual violence and the continuous raping of his aunt cannot be understood apart from John's ongoing concerns about his masculinity. Thus, although the sexual violence in John's family constitutes a major difference between John, Sam, and Zack, the masculinity challenges at school—and the boys' active responses—reflect striking similarities among the three boys.[2]

Indeed, the life stories of Sam, John, and Zack show how dominant and subordinate masculinities are constructed in and through bodily and sexual images, interactions, and practices (Connell 1995). Being constructed as a "wimp" (bodily) and a "fag" (sexually)—yet simultaneously attracted to women—Sam, John, and Zack were disallowed participation in hegemonic masculinity and sexuality at school. Consequently, the behavioral expressions activated by the contextual masculinity challenges could be directed only *outside* the school situation. It is in this sense that the bodies of the three sex offenders became party to a surrogate masculine practice that directed them toward courses of masculine social action that were physically and sexually realizable—and that could be accomplished outside the boundaries of school. These boys had a desperate need to abandon their subordinate positions and fit into the hegemonic masculine model offered by the "cool guys." For each sex offender, then, the dominant masculine practices in school were not rejected. Rather, physical and sexual subordination directed the boys toward *fixating* on a specific site, the home, and a particular form of conduct, sexual violence, where such practices could be realized. Moreover, all three sex offenders had access to less powerful people at home and therefore the means through which their bodies could attain physical and sexual expression. Given that each sex offender was removed from any type of recognized masculine status in school, the available sexual "outlet" at home was especially seductive and captivating, became an obsession, and was a powerful and pleasurable means of doing masculinity.[3] In attempting to masculinize and heterosexualize their bodies within the captivating conceptualization of "cool guy" masculinity, they engendered a powerful sense of self by "taking charge" at home and conquering girls' bodies through sexual violence. The choice to be sexually violent, then, was a situational resource in which each sex offender could be dominant, powerful, and heterosexual through bodily practice. Moreover, constructing girls as the "other" to simply "fuck" in order to "do" masculinity—concurrent with situationally constructed homophobia—is horrifyingly demonstrable in their life stories.

Unfortunately, for confidentiality reasons, I was unable to contact and interview the survivors of the sex offenders' violence. Nevertheless, we can assume from previous studies of child and adolescent rape victimization that survivors experience both short- and long-term effects, such as anxiety, depression, fear, impaired sense of self, and interpersonal difficulties (Kendall-Tackett and Marshall 1998). Moreover, the life history data reveal that prior to, during, and immediately after the sexual violence all three sex offenders perceived their crimes not as rape but as legitimate ways to "do" heterosexuality and masculinity. Thus, from the perspectives of Sam, John, and Zack, they constructed a specific type of heterosexuality: a dominating and controlling form of heterosexuality. Recall that Sam saw himself as supermasculine. He was "better" than the "cool guys" because he had complete control over the girls he babysat. John learned sexual domination: "I thought this was normal for a guy to do." And Zack "just felt like finally I was in control over somebody." In short, all three boys, in different ways, eroticized domination over a powerless "partner" as an alternative masculine practice to their inability to physically dominate the "cool guys" at school.

Thus the sex offenders' life stories challenge perspectives that conceptualize sexual violence as simply the personification of male power. All three boys unmistakably lacked masculine power—that is, vis-à-vis other boys at school—and the resulting sexual violence was motivated to realize bodily domination and power over their victims *and* to be heterosexual like the "real guys." They literally "bounced back," like a cat with nine lives, to "do" masculinity in a specific way. This conclusion in no way implies that in-school dominant boys perpetually steer clear of rape. On the contrary, involvement in powerful athletic and popular "cool guy" groups in particular school settings often facilitates sexual violence (Lefkowitz 1997; Martin and Hummer 1998; Schwartz and DeKeseredy 1997; Sanday 1990). Arguably the life stories of Sam, John, and Zack reveal the pervasiveness of adolescent male sexual violence and the complex nature of such crime. Adolescent male sexual violence is engaged in by certain dominant *and* subordinate boys, and their differing social experiences shape the contrasting forms of their sexual violence. However, criminological literature has paid little attention, if any, to the social practices of subordinate boys who have been labeled "wimp" or "sissy." Accordingly, the life stories of these three boys provide, for the first time, telling information on sexual violence by subordinate boys. We have examined the unique experiences of these three "heterosexual sissy" boys who were constructed bodily as not masculine but were nevertheless sexually attracted to girls (Hunter 1993).

Moreover, these boys' life histories add new light to, for example, perspectives that view sexual violence as learned behavior and as an extension of the "male role" in patriarchal society (Scully 1990). Such perspectives are unable to account for the varieties of masculinities constructed in relation to each other in a given milieu, as well as one's agency and the situational accomplishment of masculinities over the life course. In the life histories, however, we are able to "see" that all three boys *created* a situation in which they were in masculine control and in which they could not be rejected by "emasculating" boys and girls—no matter how their bodies appeared or acted. Recall Sam's comment: "There was no way I could get rejected." John's: "She's mine so she's gonna do what I want her to do." And Zack's: "I just felt like finally I was in control over somebody." In short, these three boys constructed a nonthreatening context in which masculinity could be performed according to the in-school dominant criteria.

Doing Assaultive Violence

For Hugh and Perry, school and family life were circumscribed by institutionalized authoritarian routine. Neither interested in nor successful at schoolwork, these two boys viewed school as irrelevant to their future and emasculating to their conception of masculinity (Willis 1977). To Hugh and Perry school, like home, was simply another milieu in which they were tyrannized by adults. Accordingly, their bodily resources empowered them to implement a physically confrontational masculinity. As such, they joined with similar working-class boys in an unstructured counterschool group that carved out a specific oppositional masculine response within the school to its overwhelming rules and unnerving authority. Their embodiment permitted them to physically resist the school and in so doing to construct behavior patterns—acting out, bullying, and fighting—that set them above the "wimps" as well as above the school. Thus, within the social setting of school, the bodies of Hugh and Perry became their primary resource for masculine power and esteem. Both boys represent the masculine "tough guy" who is, as Joyce Canaan (1998, 179) points out,

> able to occupy space because he successfully makes his might known to others. Because he can keep the other at a distance and thereby defines the situation, he is able to operate on and control this other. He has a particular kind of male power; his presence and literal staying power imply the threat of violence.

The school milieu offered all six violent boys a powerless place vis-à-vis the teachers, and each boy—in and through his body—determined how to "take it up." Rather than conform to in-school formal discipline (which Sam, John, and Zack chose to do), Hugh and Perry used their bodies in ways the sex offenders could not. They physically expressed themselves in a manner culturally idolized in the school, thereby negating any masculine insecurities developed at home. Acting out in class, for instance, is a practice that treats a teacher's insistence on right to authority as violative of their masculine rights to autonomy, independence, and control. It was this authority represented by the teacher that became a masculinity challenge for these boys, and against which Hugh and Perry constructed their in-school masculinity.

Moreover, in joining the counterschool group, Hugh and Perry began to separate themselves from the dominant masculinity and to construct an in-school opposition masculinity. Eventually they left school, finding masculine comfort in the street gang. The gang was an arena in which both boys could bodily express themselves through physical confrontation. Within the collective setting of the gang, such practices as group robbery and burglary and assaultive violence were particularly attractive, providing a public demonstration of bodily domination over and humiliation of others. Both individual and group violence were motivated by masculinity challenges ("talking shit" and "invading our territory"). Although the group process included women, Hugh and Perry constructed their masculinity through subordinating practices of women and violent interaction with them. By "slapping down" women, Hugh and Perry constituted themselves as representatives of dominant in-group masculinity.

Hugh and Perry, then, exemplify the "normal criminal" of the criminological gaze—the usual violent individuals studied by criminologists. For example, Hugh and Perry fit the profile reported in recent work on robbery, burglary, and persistent property offenders (Wright and Decker 1994, 1997; Shover 1996). Indeed, these two boys eventually became stalwart participants in the street culture that Wright, Decker, and Shover emphasize in their work; Hugh and Perry committed property crimes in part to "keep the party going." Their social existence outside school consisted exclusively of "life as party" or enjoyment of "good times," with minimal concern for obligations and commitments external to their immediate social setting (Shover 1996, 93). Life as party is a collective practice that typically includes shared consumption of alcohol and other drugs through which "party pursuers" celebrate and affirm their independence, thereby promoting "avoidance of routine work, freedom from being 'under someone's thumb,' and freedom to avoid or escape from restrictive routines" (p. 95). Moreover, because such activities are cash intensive, those with the ability to sustain them over a period of time are accorded increased masculine respect and status in the street culture. As Wright and Decker (1994, 201) argue, "To be seen as hip on the street, one must be able to keep the party going." Furthermore, part of this collective party life entails occasional involvement in individual and group violence. In the street gang, Hugh and Perry gained masculine status, reputation, and self-respect through their continued ability to "party" and by engaging in various property crimes and assaultive violence. Like the sex offenders, Hugh and Perry "bounced back" from what to them was an oppressive home and school environment and constructed a specific type of masculinity.

The Case of Lenny

Lenny's eventual physical violence presents an interesting exception to the three sex offenders and the other two assaultive offenders. Like the sex offenders, Lenny was often abused at school for his physical size and shape and for not demonstrating that he was "a man." Lenny accepted the notion that being masculine meant responding to provocation with physical violence. But because he was physically small and obese relative to the bullies, Lenny was unable to respond in such a "manly" fashion. However, this does not mean that Lenny simply accepted this powerless position. On the contrary, when taunted by physically smaller and weaker boys at school and in his neighborhood, Lenny turned to assault as a response. Lenny prudently averted retaliating against the bullies while carefully creating a situation in which his masculine domination would be "successful"—Lenny's form of "bouncing back" in a masculine way. Thus Lenny chose the hallway at school and the street in his neighborhood as appropriate sites for physical domination of other boys because in these sites the violence, he hoped, would be confirmed by his peers. Although it did not work out completely as he wished—some in the "audience" told him to "pick on" someone his own size—Lenny was able to satisfy his father's criteria for doing appropriate masculine violence. Thus his fear of being seen as a "wimp" and his resulting low masculine self-esteem motivated Lenny to deny masculinity in other "others." His agency and eventual violence can be understood only as a manifestation of in-school homophobic oppression and a strong desire to remain attached to his father.

However, Lenny's story also begs an important question: Given his in-school definition as "wimp," why did Lenny, unlike Sam, John, and Zack, not engage in sexual violence? The answer, I believe, is at least twofold. First, Lenny had access to boys who were smaller and weaker than himself—boys he could physically assault. Lenny's agency, in part, was recognizing such boys and selecting the appropriate site for his body to conduct itself in the appropriate physically masculine way. Indeed, in the hallway at school and on the street in his neighborhood, Lenny was applauded by his mentor (father) for demonstrating his physical capabilities. The sex offenders differed in that they were never able to demonstrate toughness through physical aggression. Second, Lenny's conception of sexuality and therefore masculinity differed from that of the three sex offenders. Again, the reason is twofold. First, sexuality is not important to Lenny; as he stated, one does not need to be sexual to be "cool." For Sam, John, and Zack, sexuality was a crucial component of daily life. Moreover, because his brother was gay and Lenny recognized him as masculine, heterosexuality was not as connected to masculinity as it is for Sam, John, and Zack. Second, Lenny's father emphasized, and Lenny accepted, that masculinity is not related to violence against women—"it's okay to hit boys but not girls." Therefore bodily control of girls was conceptualized as outside the realm of masculine practice. Consequently, Lenny was defined socially as a "heterosexual sissy" who used *physical* violence—rather than *sexual* violence—in an attempt to nullify his subordinate masculine status at school.

Conclusion

By reason of their interactions at home and in the culture of cruelty at school, all six violent boys launched masculinities that emphasized, in particular, physically standing up to threat. It was their differing abilities to fulfill such predispositions at school—and their subsequent bodily and sexual subordination (Sam, John, Zack, and Lenny) or superordination (Hugh and Perry)—that focused their interests and behavior in the specific direction of sexual violence (Sam, John, and Zack) or assaultive violence (Hugh, Perry, and Lenny). Masculinity grew particularly salient for all six boys as the social situation of the school defined both physical and sexual performance as essential criteria for "doing masculinity." Thus these dominant criteria—within the context of a body either able or unable to construct such criteria—directed the boys' ultimate choices of a specific type of violence and victimization. The three sex offenders chose private and solitary sexual violence that repeatedly victimized the same person. Hugh, Perry, and Lenny chose public and social assaultive violence that chiefly victimized strangers or acquaintances. Furthermore, the sex offenders were sexual violence "specialists." Hugh and Perry were "versatile" in their criminal endeavors and never engaged in sexual violence, and Lenny was an assaultive "specialist" who never engaged in any other type of violence or in any type of property crime.

Although all six white working-class teenage boys realized their behavior was held accountable to others, the sex and assaultive offenders produced specific but different types of masculine configurations through the use of contrasting forms of violence. These different types of masculinities emerged from practices that reflected different bodily resources. Hugh and Perry constructed opposition masculinities that, though individual, occurred within the context of a collective masculine project. Sam, John, Zack, and Lenny attempted to invalidate their subordinate masculine statuses in school through personal reconstructions of self and not as part of a shared, collective project.

Although different in these crucial ways, the sex and assaultive offenders are similar in that their differing forms of violence rely on bodily deployment and performance. Each boy, in his individually telling way, ex-

ercised power over other bodies. Hugh and Perry subordinated and oppressed females ("slapping them down") and males (for "talking shit"
and invading their turf) through *assaultive* violence. Lenny subordinated
and oppressed "other" males (for teasing him and challenging him to a
fight) through *assaultive* violence. Sam, John, and Zack subordinated and
oppressed females (and one male) through *sexual* violence. The sex and
assaultive offenders experienced their everyday worlds from specific
bodily positions and their bodies, in turn, entered negotiated social interactions and shaped future social practices. For all these boys, their sense
of masculinity was fashioned by their bodily relations in school and their
bodies—as resources for social action—restrained or facilitated possible
masculine agency and subsequent practice.

Let us now turn our attention to the nonviolent boys.

NOTES

1. Boys who are physically small yet participate in athletics and in popular
cliques are much less likely to be bullied at school (Thorne 1993; Martin 1996).

2. This is not to dismiss the importance of physical, sexual, and emotional
violence against children in families. Rather, it is to suggest that we should
not let this impede the search for other factors that may possibly be more
strongly associated with adolescent male sexual violence.

3. Although Sam participated in other masculine practices at home—such
as helping his dad with his tools—these practices were contextually inappropriate for resolving the masculinity challenges at school (e.g., they did not involve proper bodily and sexual practices). For John and Zack, alternative
masculine resources were nonexistent at home.

5

Jerry, Dennis, and Alan

In this chapter I present the life stories of Jerry (age 17), Dennis (age 17), and Alan (age 18). All three boys are "nonviolent" because (1) they had not admitted committing nor had been formally charged with committing a violent offense or (2) they had admitted engaging in violence (but had never been formally charged) for a brief period early in their life (at a young age) and thereafter adopted an exclusively nonviolent pattern of behavior. One boy (Dennis) grew up in a violent home; the other two (Jerry and Alan) grew up in nonviolent homes. Analogous to the life stories presented in Chapters 2 and 3, these three case studies are opportunities for examining similarities and differences between a boy raised in a violent family who never engaged in violence and boys reared in nonviolent families who eventually became entirely nonviolent. We begin with Jerry.

Jerry

Jerry was a tall, slightly overweight seventeen-year-old who displayed considerable maturity and self-reliance. He presented the relaxed deportment of a happy and at-ease individual who engaged easily in conversation with an adult; we could have discussed his life for days.

Jerry lives in a small house located in the center of a working-class town. His earliest memory is living alone with his mother, who had separated from his father because of his alcohol abuse. To make ends meet, Jerry's mother worked two jobs in the unskilled-labor market. Early on Jerry felt very close to his mother. Although she worked a lot, he was proud of the fact that "she managed to keep things together for us."

While his mother worked, Jerry was cared for by several different couples who were friends of the family. Depending on the day of the week and the time of day, Jerry would stay with one or another of the couples. Although he rotated among "babysitting" families, he has only fond memories of the many adults who cared for him: "They were all great. I had a lot of fun with all of them."

Around the age of six Jerry met his biological father for the first time. He explained to me how this meeting emerged:

> I had always asked, "Hey, where is Dad?" 'cause I always saw these kids with their dad. My mom is always really honest with me. That's the way we've always been, really straightforward with each other. She told me that he was a recovering alcoholic and that maybe someday I'd see him. Finally she called my grandfather and found out where my dad was, and called him, and they set up a thing where he came over to the house.

Jerry thought it was "really cool" when he first met his father because they had a wonderful time together; they went for a walk in the park and spent the entire afternoon side by side as one. Before Jerry's father left that day "we made plans to get back together soon." And it was not long after this first meeting with his father that Jerry's parents actually reconciled and all three began living under the same roof. This was exciting to Jerry because now he was like the other kids—he had both a mother and a father, and he loved his father immensely.

Jerry's father owned a small business in the unskilled manual-labor market and "worked very hard at it." He worked full-time during the day and was extremely tired when he came home in the afternoon. Nevertheless, "we'd play games and watch TV and stuff like that. He'd take me places and we'd just hang out together." When I asked Jerry who his heroes were when he was in elementary school, he stated:

> My dad for one of them because he did really hard work and everything. So that made me pretty proud of him. I always respected people that did hard work—my grandfather, great grandfather, those kinds of folks.
> *Q. What was it about hard work that impressed you?*
>   A. Well, when you've finished hard work it really shows that you have done something.
> *Q. Did that have a masculine image to you?*
>   A. Not really, because my mom worked hard at two jobs and I knew she was working hard to keep the family up.

Q. What did you want to be when you grew up?
   A. I wanted to be like my dad and mom: a hard worker at something I liked to do.

This closeness, with his father in particular, nourished Jerry's idea of future labor-force participation: Jerry wants to have a similar business after finishing high school and work hard at it. "If I start my business right out of school and I do it smart, by learning from dad's mistakes that he's made, I can go on to have a wicked business."

Jerry was also extremely pleased and proud that his father overcame addiction to alcohol. Indeed, the two were so close that Jerry would attend the "alcohol rehab" meetings with his father, and then the two would talk after the meeting. Jerry has affectionate memories not only of his father speaking up at the meetings but also of the special talks afterward. In particular, his father always expressed to Jerry during these conversations that it was not Jerry's fault that he became an alcoholic— Jerry's father took full responsibility for his addiction.

Because Jerry's father was contributing economically to the household, his mother was able to quit one of her two jobs and had time to pursue other interests (e.g., she enrolled part-time at a local university, where she took classes now and then based on personal interests).

Despite these positive developments, Jerry's parents seemed unable to get along with each other. Their difficulties were not related to his father's past problems with alcohol—he remained alcohol free—or his mother's attending university. Rather, their problems centered on financial issues and consisted of verbal battles—never any physical violence—between the two.

Jerry discussed with both parents the issues involved and the nature of the arguments; they consistently stated that the arguments were not Jerry's fault but only reflected an inability to work out financial matters. "There never was anything negative towards me from my parents, always positive things." Although these arguments constituted one of the most distressing events in Jerry's family life, his parents always protected Jerry from responsibility for their problems. In fact, Jerry and his parents were very "connected." Jerry experienced a warm and affectionate relationship with both. "We did everything together. We'd go cross-country skiing, we'd go camping, go on hikes—we were quite an outdoor family." Jerry went hunting and fishing with his dad, helped his mom and dad in the kitchen, and helped his mom in the garden. "I always liked being in the kitchen" and "there was this wonderful garden that me and my mom would be in together."

When Jerry was in elementary school and junior high school, he was responsible for some of the household chores, such as emptying the garbage, getting wood, feeding the pets, setting the table, cutting the lawn, and helping with the cooking and cleaning. Both parents worked together to cook the evening meal. Jerry remembers especially that sometimes "I'd get home from school and I could smell just-baked pies as I walked up the driveway. There would like be three pies on the table that my dad baked. And I'd be like, oh yeah!" Although his father worked at a "masculine" job and his mother at a "feminine" job, at home Jerry observed and participated in both "masculine" and "feminine" forms of domestic labor.

Nevertheless, Jerry never particularly liked chores, and frequently performed them in a "real half-ass way." Although his parents would be upset with him for his performance of these duties, he was never disciplined harshly.

> They would never send me to my room or anything like that. They'd take stuff away, you know, like no radio in my room. Or they'd threaten me that I couldn't do certain stuff on weekends.

Jerry was never spanked by either parent. Although he clearly identified with his father, Jerry's mother also had a major influence on him. His parents' participation in household labor—as well as their renunciation of interpersonal physical violence—defined for him an alternative form of masculinity that differed from the hegemonic model. And Jerry seemed to adopt what was offered.

For Jerry, school was not as congenial a place as home. He was an average student. From elementary school on through high school Jerry was the target of consistent verbal abuse for being overweight. "I was called 'chubby' and 'fat ass' a lot. I was laughed at, pushed around, and it would really drag me down." Indeed, because of the comments from kids at school Jerry did not like to go to school or to be seen in public because he accepted the way others characterized his body. "I didn't like going out in public because I felt small and insecure. I was average height but fat. I did a lot of stuff by myself and didn't go out a lot."

Q. You were very concerned about the way you looked?

A. Well, as a kid you're always concerned about your physical looks. And I was very concerned about how people saw me and the way I saw myself.

Q. Can you expand on that a little for me?

A. Oh, just really low self-esteem, just a bad self-image of myself. I didn't like myself if that's the way other people saw me. I was big outside but I felt small inside.

As a result of peer abuse and acute concern over his body, Jerry developed a painful lack of masculine self-esteem. Consequently, in third grade he became involved in a number of "fistfights." These fights were simply part of what Jerry labeled "playground business," which he defined as "some kid does something and the other kid takes it as he has insulted him, so he goes up and hits the kid for insulting him. That's how kids in my grade school handled business on the playground." Being teased and bullied made Jerry feel subordinate, insecure, and small. So he would respond according to the playground definition of appropriately handling such "business." "Kids would bully me and then I'd feel better by bullying other kids. If I got bullied, then I had to put someone down by beating the shit out of him." If Jerry did not bully or fight back, he would be called a wimp: "Kids would keep bullying me." Jerry wanted to be "tough" in front of the other kids, so he got into eight fights that year.

Q. Did you fight back against the kids who bullied you?

A. Yeah, sometimes, and sometimes I'd go after other kids.

Q. How did that make you feel?

A. It made me feel that if I could bring somebody else down, then I would be higher than them and that was better.

Q. You beat up some kids?

A. Oh, yeah. I lost some and won some.

I asked Jerry if he discussed this peer abuse and fighting with either parent, and he said "of course." In fact, all three—Mom, Dad, and Jerry—discussed the issue together after his first fight: "They sat me down and had a nice talk with me. They were like, 'Oh, we're really sorry,' and they told me it wasn't my fault when I was bullied and everything, and just to next time turn my back. Not to fight."

Q. Your parents didn't tell you to bully back or fight back?

A. No, my mom and dad never said that. My mom is against that, you know, the macho thing about guys that have to puff themselves all up and everything.

Q. Did your parents teach you to handle these kinds of problems in a nonviolent way?

A. Yeah. My mom wanted me to see that you didn't have to do that and my dad is the same way. We talked about it quite a bit. My parents would say, "It's the other kid's problem. There's something wrong with kids that bully kids."

At first Jerry did not accept his parents' suggestion and continued to respond in a physically violent way at school. Jerry explained that he could not simply "walk away" because "you have to show kids you're not afraid to do it. My mom and dad didn't understand what it was like." The following extended dialogue demonstrates how Jerry eventually accepted a nonviolent response to these challenges at school:

Q. But after each fight you talked to your parents about it?

A. Oh, yeah. We've always had a very open relationship.

Q. Both parents were telling you to just walk away, but at the same time you felt you could not because you had to show other kids that you were tough?

A. Right. My mom and dad said [to] walk away and the kids on the playground said show that you are tough. It was very confusing for a little kid.

Q. How did you resolve this dilemma?

A. My mom and dad had more and more of these talks with me, and around the fifth grade what they were saying began to sink in.

Q. It was the persistence of your parents then that changed your mind?

A. Yeah, and I did kind of experiments at school where if a kid started saying stuff I would just walk away. And that's when it really started to sink in. It was nice, and I'd come home and say to my parents, "Hey, you guys are right."

Q. When you walked away didn't the kids continue to bully and tease you?

A. Yeah, but I could deal with it because I knew that I wasn't going to get into trouble. Knowing that if they get caught telling me I'm a "wimp" and "fat ass" that they are going to be the one's in trouble. That felt good.

Q. But how did you deal with the idea that you may still be a wimp because you didn't fight back?

A. It was the talks with my parents. They'd reassure me that you were stronger to walk away than to put up your dukes and fight about it. And then I did that and I started to understand that "hey, they're right and it works."

Jerry indicated that his parents' emphasis on solving interpersonal problems in a nonviolent manner probably had something to do with the fact that his mother had subscribed to *Ms.* magazine and was "into the whole feminist thing." While attending part-time classes, Jerry's mother met a number of women and began to participate in a feminist support group. "There's like four or five women that she sees once or twice a month."

Q. Did your mother introduce you to some feminist ideas?

A. A couple of things 'cause she was taking women's studies classes.

Q. Did your mother teach you about how to handle the bullying?

A. Yeah. She'd be like, "Just brush it off." So that's how I kind of have gotten around it. It's just brushing it off. You know, I would say to myself, "there must be something wrong with this kid if they feel they have to make fun of me."

Q. So it was interaction with your mother that convinced you not to fight back when bullied?

A. Right. But Dad *and* Mom never encouraged fighting. I learned from them that if I was picked on I should find a different way to respond. Both Mom and Dad said that.

Despite the fact that Jerry continued to be the victim of peer abuse, these discussions with his parents convinced him to never again respond by fighting. Instead, he would simply walk away. "Usually it resolves itself. You just walk away and the kid doesn't even say anything to you because he can't get a rise out of you." Jerry concluded that this is the best way to handle such a situation. He felt confident doing it this way because, although the bully continues "as you're walking away, later it's like you just don't even acknowledge that he's there."

Jerry first learned about sexuality in seventh grade. "I was snooping around the house one day and I found that my parents had the *Joy of Sex* books, and so I looked at them a lot." He also heard from kids at school about heterosexuality. "Guys would talk about it all the time—having sex and stuff with girls." He had two girlfriends in junior high school, one in seventh grade and one in eighth grade; neither friendship progressed beyond "going out on dates." Jerry eventually mentioned the books to his parents and several times they looked through them together. On one occasion Jerry and his parents were scanning through the books when they "came to these two girls that were having sex and I was like 'what's this?'" Jerry's parents explained that the women were lesbians and that "some people were into that kind of thing." When they told him that his sexual orientation was "up to him," he told his parents that he "always liked the female body." He also learned at this time that his two older cousins were gay. Jerry said that he and his mother frequently have tea with several gay and lesbian friends. In any event, there was arguably no "emphasis"—simply "balance."

Although successful in teaching Jerry how to handle interpersonal problems at school in a nonconflictual way, his parents continued to disagree over family finances. Indeed, these disagreements escalated to the point where they decided that divorce was the only option. Consequently, when Jerry was in the sixth grade his father moved out of the house. Jerry was extremely sad about the divorce but, as he put it, "there was still love and affection from both of them. It just wasn't at the same time." He continued to spend considerable time with both parents on a regular basis. "They'd always say, 'we're having our own problems and it's not your fault.'" Jerry never felt he was the cause of the divorce.

Jerry lived with his mother and visited his father on weekends until he was fifteen. Everything was fine in Jerry's life until he became what he describes as "lazy around the house." He refused to do most of the chores his mother asked him to do because "I had my own things I wanted to do. I wanted to hang out with my friends and go places, and she didn't want me to do that because she needed help at home and she was working." During Jerry's seventh- and eighth-grade years his mother was not home when he returned from school because of her work. Jerry was supposed to use this time for homework and chores. He would usually do his homework but only a few chores, and then he would play with his friends. Jerry liked his friends because "they accepted me for who I was."

Q. What did you like to do with your friends?

A. Ride snowmobiles and practice shooting guns. We had fun together 'cause we never teased or fought.

Q. But you didn't do your chores?

A. Right. I'd slack off. I wouldn't do the dishes, walk the dog. I'd just watch TV or hang out with my friends, because I didn't want to do my chores. I was irresponsible.

Q. And your mother would continue to ask you to help out with the household duties?

A. Yeah. She'd say, "It's important that you learn to do this now, because when you're older there isn't going to be anybody that wants to take care of you." And I was like, "Whatever. I'll find somebody." And then she just kept nagging me and getting mad at me because I was lazy. So I finally told her "I want to move in with Dad."

Jerry moved in with his dad during the early part of his freshman year in high school. The peer abuse persisted in high school but Jerry never responded in a violent way. The "walking away" reaction continued to work and he felt comfortable using it. The most frequent verbal abuse Jerry experienced in high school is being "called a fag a lot, and queer, and anything pertaining to being homosexual. So I just shrug it off. I could yell at the kid or something, but there's no point. He is just going to be narrow-minded about it. So I just turn my back on it instead of putting up the dukes."

Jerry is abused mostly by the "popular guys." As he puts it, "The tough guys, the athletes, the macho guys." When I asked Jerry if he wanted to be like the "popular guys" he said, "At first I did. But then Mom and Dad told me, 'Just be your own person.' And that had a lot of influence on me. Plus I never really liked sports."

Q. You never liked sports?

A. Not really organized sports. I liked playing hockey, but not for a team.

Q. You just didn't want to participate in the organized aspect of sports?

A. You know in high school I see the locker room camaraderie. They walk around and snap each other's asses with towels and everything. I'm not really interested in that. And there is a lot of macho crap that goes on in the locker room and everything, and I just don't want to be part of that.

Q. Tell me about the other cliques in your high school.

A. The jocks are the popular guys because they get in the news for accomplishments they make in sports. It's like, "Hey, did you see so and so in the news the other day?" And then there are the brains which most people ignore. And then there are the loaders.

Q. What are loaders?

A. They are the mostly druggies. They're into pot and stuff. And then there are the homies or G-funks, because G is for gangsta. The G-funks think they're the tough guys.

Q. Which group are you in?

A. I'm not in a group. I have some friends that are loaders; we are kinda the laid-back crowd. But I'm not in any group 'cause it's like they all have something to prove. I've got nothing to prove. I am who I am, and if they don't like it—too bad.

Jerry also stated that there are numerous "feminine boys" in his school and, not surprisingly, "some" homophobia as well. Most people ignore these boys but occasionally they call them "fags."

Q. Are these boys gay?

A. I don't know if they are gay but they are kinda feminine. I get along with them real well but some guys constantly call them names like "fag" and "queer." I accept that some people are just like that.

Q. But you consider yourself heterosexual?

A. Yeah. I just never had a sexual interest in guys. When I was younger I liked to play with my friends but I like never saw it in a sexual way. It wasn't until around seventh grade that I started to like girls. I became interested in their body then.

In high school Jerry was yet to have a date (he described himself as a "virgin") but had numerous girl *friends*. "There are a bunch of girls at school that I get along with. I treat them just like anybody else, just like my friends. We talk about what's going on in life."

Q. Do you ever hear kids at school talking about engaging in sex?

A. Oh, yeah. I hear that a lot. But it's like, "That's real tacky." If somebody is going to brag about that then I'm sorry to hear it. There is more to life than getting a piece of ass.

Q. So sexuality isn't something that is important to you?

A. I think sex is pretty much important to everybody. It's part of life, but not right now. I'm more interested in bringing my grades up in school than having sex.

Q. What are your plans after high school?
A. I'm going to have a family. I'm going to enjoy raising my kids. There are just so many things out there that I want to do that seem like fun. I'd love to race motorcycles. I'd love to have a dogsled team. There are just so many things out there that I'd love to do. I'm gonna start a business like Dad's, and then who knows where I could go!

Despite frequent parental verbal battles and the ensuing divorce, Jerry grew up in a warm, affectionate, and nonviolent home. His parents were his "heroes," for whom he had immense respect and love. Before discussing physical violence with his parents, during his third-grade year, Jerry had accepted as legitimate and had consequently practiced forms of "playground" physical violence. The victim of continuous peer abuse regarding his body size, and feeling insecure and small inside, Jerry followed the playground masculine "script" of bullying and fighting back. Nevertheless, because of the open relationship he has with his parents, he immediately and consistently discussed these violent events with them. The outcome was that Jerry's parents convinced him, and his own "experiments" at school demonstrated to him, that an alternative response—walking away—was a much more secure and successful answer to the playground challenges. Moreover, Jerry "hung out" with numerous boys and girls who were "laid back" and accepted him for "who I am." Thus, through interaction at home and at school, Jerry was able to counteract his bodily and masculine insecurities and change his working-class masculinity from one that emphasized physical violence to one that emphasized fishing, hunting, helping out with the domestic chores, working in the paid-labor market, and nonviolence.

Dennis

Dennis was a tall and remarkably slim seventeen-year-old who grew up with his biological mother and father in the center of a working-class town. The family owned a small ranch house in a neighborhood with "lots of kids." Dennis's earliest memory is of his father buying him a "dirt bike" when he was five years old. "My first bike was not a regular bike; it was a dirt bike, and I thought that was real cool. I got a dirt bike with little training wheels on it, which was really great." His father taught him how to ride the bike. This relationship between Dennis and his father, as well as the "dirt bike," was significant throughout his childhood.

Before he entered junior high school, Dennis had a warm and affectionate relationship with both parents. His mother stayed home after Dennis
was born and throughout his elementary school years. (After he started
junior high, she began to work full-time outside the household in the unskilled-labor market.) During his elementary school years, when Dennis
spent much time with both parents, his mother taught him "intellectual
things" by playing board games with him and reading to him each night
before going to bed. His father—who worked full-time in the skilled-
labor market—read to him, played board games with him, and in addition taught him how to become an "expert" at riding "dirt bikes." Dennis's father also taught him how to fish and all about the workings of an
automobile. "He liked to go fishing and fix cars, and so he showed me
how to do it. And he liked to do mostly outdoor stuff with me."

There was a nontraditional gender division of labor in Dennis's household. Both parents were equally responsible for the cooking, cleaning,
laundry, and shopping. Dennis helped out as much as he could. His major responsibility was to "take out the trash" and help his father "fix stuff
around the house and work on cars and dirt bikes." Prior to entering junior high, Dennis had a home life that was cooperative, pleasant, genial,
and warm. It deemphasized separate gendered spheres into "men's
work" and "women's work." During this time Dennis's father was the
major influence for masculinity in his life. "I didn't know what a 'real
man' was then but I sure thought my father was cool—I wanted to be like
him when I got bigger."

School was a less benign environment than home for Dennis. Following first grade he was held back a year and felt resentment toward his
mother because she and the school principal "were talking it over, and I
was angry 'cause my mom had the choice of saying I can go to the second
grade or stay back. So she had a choice and she said 'stay back.'" Although Dennis understood her reasoning later, at the time it was frustrat-
ing because he had to make new friends. "All my friends went ahead and
I was left back, so I had to make new friends. That was hard."

Eventually Dennis acquired several friends in his repeat grade, and
they would do "normal things" together—"play on the playground, going on slides and stuff, and things like that." This was a happy time for
Dennis. He spent "a lot of time with my friends playing on the playground and riding dirt bikes." He was an average student who had little
interest in school except for recess. "I just wanted to play with my friends
'cause I didn't really like school."

When Dennis advanced from elementary to junior high school, he noticed a change in his father's behavior. In particular, he "started to really boss me and my mom around a lot. He really made every decision for my mom and told us what to do." Dennis's father had not been dominating and controlling in the past—generally there was equality between mother and father regarding decisionmaking—and so this new behavior pattern seemed odd to him. Before Dennis started attending junior high school, neither parent had spanked him when he misbehaved. When I asked him how they disciplined him, Dennis stated, "I'd be sent to my room or I had to stand in the corner for a while." Later, however, Dennis's father became physically violent toward him: "Once I got spanked by my father so hard that it left a big red handprint on my butt." Dennis's mother, however, never spanked him; in fact, she attempted to stop his father from doing it. The unfortunate result was that Dennis's father became extremely violent toward her as well. Dennis offered the following explanation for the changed family environment:

My father made all the decisions and my mom started realizing that she should make some decisions, and she started to make some and he started to change a lot. They would argue a lot and yell at each other, and he would go around and slam doors. He would hit her, and he would spy on her sometimes because he thought she was cheating on him. So he would hide in closets and tap phones to see if she would say anything on the phone or meet people.

Q. *Did your father ever catch her doing anything wrong?*

A. No. She was a great wife. She never cheated on him and she had a job, and she did all the work around the house now.

In addition, Dennis's father would occasionally engage in other forms of violence toward his son. Dennis remembers one incident that took place while he was watching TV. His father came into the room and pushed him hard over the back of the rocking chair in which he was sitting. It all happened so quickly that he had no clue as to what had transpired until his head hit the floor. Dennis sustained no permanent injury but did have "quite a headache" from it for some time. More importantly, however, he was confused as to why his father would engage in such uncanny conduct: "He came home and he was angry, and he saw me there watching TV. And I was going back and forth in the rocking chair, and he just grabbed the back of the chair and threw me down."

Dennis and his father periodically fished and rode dirt bikes together, but it was not the same as it was in the past. Dennis was less and less interested in doing these things with his father because "he would like watch me real close to see if I made a mistake or did somethin' wrong, and if I did he would like really yell at me and shake his head." Indeed, the father would hug Dennis only when he accomplished some task in a way his father approved. For example, "When I caught a big fish he would hug me. Only times like that." His father also wanted him to enter dirt bike races, but he was afraid of "failing in front of him" and thus showed no interest. His father became intensely upset and he made "me feel bad about that. I was real nervous around him."

The father's changed behavior had a detrimental effect on Dennis's masculine self-esteem. Whereas earlier he felt proud of his father for being a "cool" guy, now he lived in a household in which he was frightened of his "hero." "He scared me, and I would go to my room when he would be coming home from work. I was like afraid to do stuff around him. I was like real sad 'cause I never did anything right but made him mad." I asked Dennis if he talked to his mother about his father and he responded, "Yeah, she was nice to me and tried to cheer me up. She hugged me and stuff, and always told my father he was wrong. She made me feel better."

Eventually the screaming arguments, extreme jealousy, physical violence, and overall patriarchal presence of Dennis's father became intolerable, and his mother divorced his father when Dennis was about ten years old. As his father left the house, Dennis remembered, "the last thing he said to my mom and me was that he hated us." Dennis never saw his father again. Like Jerry, Dennis learned from his mother that his father's violent behavior and the ensuing divorce were not his fault. "After he left she told me that it wasn't my fault that he was mean to me and they were divorcing. But I wasn't sad he was gone." Comfort from his mother helped minimize Dennis's developing lack of masculine self-esteem at home.

Dennis did "pretty well" in junior high. "I didn't flunk anything, and got some As and Bs. I met a lot of friends like I did in elementary school. I always got along with teachers. I never got in trouble in school. I always raised my hand and tried to participate in class." However, he did not like the "cooler kids" because they frequently abused him verbally. Dennis "hung out" with the "regular kids," and he and his friends never experienced major conflicts. However, Dennis was subjected to persistent verbal abuse because of his body size and shape—the "cool guys" would call him "skinny," "bean," "stork legs," "bony," and "weakling." He found the name-calling agonizing and unbearable. I asked Dennis if he discussed this peer abuse with his parents:

A. I did. I talked to my mom about it. She just told me that it didn't count because they don't live my life so I shouldn't bother with them.
Q. *How did she tell you to respond?*
A. Like I did. I should walk away or tell a teacher.
Q. *Did that work out okay?*
A. Yeah.
Q. *How about your father? Did you talk to him about the teasing and bullying before the divorce?*
A. No, because I knew he would probably have told me to go after them. You know, he would have wanted me to get involved and stick up for myself. So if I didn't let him know about it, then I wouldn't let him down. I knew I wouldn't want to fight.
Q. *Why not?*
A. I was skinny and I wasn't very strong at that time. I knew that if I fought that I would get beat up.
Q. *How did that make you feel?*
A. Like a "wimp" and a "weakling." Like I said, I hated myself because I couldn't fight.
Q. *But your mom told you to simply walk away?*
A. Right. So what's the point of getting beat up instead of walking away? I don't care what they say as long as I don't get hurt. So when they called me names I walked away like she said. I did that even when they said things about me when I was walking away. It didn't matter.
Q. *How did you deal with being called a "wimp" as you walked away?*
A. It made me upset, and I tried to fit in the cool crowd and dress like them, listen to the same music—but it didn't work out too well. They just started calling me "copy cat." So I just went back to who I was.
Q. *Was that bothersome to you?*
A. Yeah, it was. But I had my own friends and we did things after school. So I just spent time with them and I forgot about the cool crowd.

Dennis also spent considerable time with his mother. "I would help her around the house as much as I could. I always had a strong connection with my mom, so I always liked to spend a lot of time with her." I asked

Dennis for some examples of what he and his mother would do together. "If she was doing the dishes, I would dry, or if she was vacuuming, I would take all the junk off the floor. Stuff like that."

Dennis first learned about sexuality in junior high school. "We had this course in sixth grade that taught about sex and the human body. We would watch films and talk about it in class and we would read about it." And Dennis heard the popular kids talking about engaging in heterosexuality and observed them labeling certain boys "fag" and "queer." "A lot of kids really made fun of other kids because they thought they were gay. They called them 'queer' and 'fag' because of the way they would walk and talk—so they assumed they were gay. They didn't accept them. But it never bothered me; they could live their own life." Dennis said he learned of the differences between heterosexuality and homosexuality by observing these interactions in school and in sex ed class. "Kids would bring it up a lot during sex ed." Although he considered himself heterosexual, he did not have a "real girlfriend" in junior high school. "I had a lot of girls that were my friends and we spent a lot of time together, but no girlfriends."

Although many of the popular kids bragged about engaging in intercourse, Dennis did not believe much of the "sex talk" at school. And it did not bother him that he was not "doing it" because "a lot of my friends said they didn't either, so I didn't feel bad about not having sex." Moreover, being masculine like the "cool guy jocks" was not important to Dennis because he noticed that many "of my girl friends didn't really care like how many pounds you can lift and stuff." In addition, although the popular kids called him "skinny" and ridiculed him about his body, "all my friends didn't really care how skinny I was. It really didn't make a difference to them so it really didn't make any difference to me."

When Dennis entered high school, some of the abuse continued. For example, if he decided to speak up in class he frequently made mistakes or said "something stupid." Invariably, someone in the class would make fun of him and many classmates would laugh out loud. In addition, the popular guys continued to call him "wimp" and "skinny." He especially disliked gym class because he had to take his shirt off and also had to wear shorts. His ribcage was easily visible and kids would make fun of his entire body, especially his legs. This was especially troubling to Dennis. "It hurt me because I felt bad about my body. But also it restricted me in some areas because I wouldn't dare to cross a hall or go to some areas at school 'cause the trouble kids were there."

Despite this abusive behavior, Dennis continued to "walk away" without verbally retaliating or physically fighting back. This seemed to work: As he progressed through high school, he noticed fewer and fewer degrading comments directed at him from the "cool guys." This relief from abuse may also have occurred because Dennis spent most of his time with friends—who never made comments about body size and shape—and avoided, as much as possible, the "cool crowd."

The year Dennis entered high school his mother met a "new man." Soon they fell in love and he moved into the house. Dennis liked "Dad" (what he called him) very much ("he is a father figure to me") because he helped Dennis with many things. "Whenever I need help with anything he is always there for me. He taught me how to play tennis; we go swimming; and we all go on trips together. He's like a real dad." There were no arguments between his mother and his "dad" ("they love each other"), and "Dad," like Mom, was nonviolent. Indeed, "dad" supported mother's position that violence was never the appropriate response to peer abuse. "Dad says like Mom that I should just walk away. That you are a better person to do it like that."

Dennis had no girlfriend until he entered high school. "We only kiss and things like that; we never go any further than that." He also identified five girls as his friends, with whom he "hung out" (along with some boys) on weekends. They spent most of their time at the local mall but also went to movies, to clubs, and to the park. Finally, Dennis found a part-time job and saved his money to buy a car.

In sum, we know that Dennis experienced childhood with warm and affectionate parents. Indeed, he wanted to grow up and be like his biological father, who taught him traditional masculine practices such as fishing, fixing cars, and riding dirt bikes. About the same time Dennis entered junior high school, however, his father became controlling and violent toward both him and his mother, lowering Dennis' self-esteem. Nevertheless, Dennis coped with the physical and psychological pain caused by his dictatorial and disparaging father until his mother divorced him. She assiduously assured Dennis that the violence was not his fault. Dennis seemed not at all dismayed when his father left and likewise lost interest in the practices associated with his father—fishing, fixing cars, and riding dirt bikes. Dennis continued to experience peer abuse at school over his body shape and size. Although he wanted to respond to these events by fighting back, he concluded that most likely the bully would "beat him up" because he was so "skinny." Thus Dennis attempted to "fit in" with the "cool crowd" but suffered their continued rejection. Once again his mom offered a welcoming ear and Dennis enjoyed helping her with the housework. She continued to teach him—reinforced by his "dad"—to simply walk away from the abuse. This strategy seemed to work. Moreover, Dennis immersed himself in a network of male and female friends who accepted his body for what it was and deemphasized sexual intercourse, masculine strength, and verbal and physical violence. Thus, like Jerry, through interaction at home and school, Dennis grew more self-confident and validated a nonviolent form of masculinity.

Alan

Alan was eighteen years old, of average height, solid, and muscular. He was exuberant—the personification of "the boy next door"—and beamed with self-confidence. He lived with his biological mother and father in the house his parents had built before he was born. Alan was the youngest of five children; he had two older brothers and two older sisters who no longer lived at home. Both parents worked full-time in the unskilled-labor market. Alan viewed neither parent as "primary"—he had equal contact with both "because if we did anything we did it together. My time was equally spent with both of them." When I asked Alan what he did with his parents when he was growing up, he stated, "We would do normal things. We'd go to the beach; we'd go camping all the time because my father is an outdoor kind of guy. We'd always have Sunday suppers." Indeed, the everyday evening meal was extremely important to Alan's family interaction. Every day the entire family would eat "supper" together at five o'clock. "Our whole family would sit at the table and that was a fine time. It was fine for me to see us sitting at the table talking about things we did that day. It was always fine conversation."

Although his mother worked full-time outside the home, Alan grew up in a family that maintained a traditional gender division of labor. His mother always did most of the domestic labor, and "me and my sisters and brothers helped my mother out." Alan's mother continued to do all the cooking and cleaning; his sisters (when living at home) would do the laundry. Alan and his brothers (when living at home) would take out the garbage, mow the lawn, and shovel the snow. "My father didn't do any of the household chores" because "he is kind of the old-fashioned kind of guy. He'd come home, and my mother would have supper ready and the house would be clean for him."

Although Alan's father had the ultimate power in the house, the kids were disciplined equally by both parents. "We weren't afraid of my father and my mother because we knew they wouldn't hit us. They would ground us if we were bad. We listened to my father but we knew behind the scenes that my mother was going to do the same thing anyway." Alan was never spanked or yelled at. Instead, his parents used a variety of nonviolent means to reprimand their children. Alan viewed his family life as consistently warm, affectionate, and nonconflictual: "I got hugs and kisses all the time from both Mom and Dad. I think my parents are great." Indeed, Alan's parents articulated their opposition to any type of physical violence in the home. "They would make comments about what we would be watching on TV. They would say 'That's horrible,' and stuff like that. They'd be reading the paper and say, 'I can't believe some guy would break a bottle over some guy's head.'" Alan's parents always expressed to him that he should "never hit anyone. My father would say, 'You hit someone and I will hit you, and then you'll see how it feels.' So I like stayed away from violence."

Although physical violence was disdained as a defining characteristic of masculinity for Alan at home, his interaction in the family also entailed explicit messages endorsing hegemonic masculinity. For example, his parents often told him, "Don't do that kind of thing, that's sissy stuff." This type of remark, coming from two people highly respected by Alan, led him to scrutinize the practices of his brothers and eschew those of his sisters, thereby escaping being called a "sissy" within the confines of his family:

I followed my big brothers. I just watched what my sisters were doing. And then I watched what my brothers were doing, because I didn't want to do what my sisters were doing. So I did what my brothers were doing—sports and stuff. I saw my sisters playing with Barbie, so I said, "I shouldn't be going that way." So I played with G.I. Joe instead. You know, like that.

Although Alan "loved" elementary school, he "hated to get up and go" in the mornings. At school he was an average student: "I got Cs and Bs. I didn't start to smarten up until high school." Elementary school was important to Alan only because he had "kids there to play with, but as a learning thing it wasn't important. I wasn't there to learn, just there to be with my friends." Alan got along with everyone, including the teachers.

"The only disruptive thing I did in school was that I was talkative in class. That's the only thing." Alan was never teased or bullied in elementary school and, although he taunted a few students several times, "it was jokingly among my friends. I stayed away from mean teasing." Alan had many friends in both elementary school and junior high; on weekends he would play with his neighborhood friends in a tree fort they had built. In addition, Alan spent a lot of his time playing sports, "like basketball and football."

Notwithstanding, when Alan went to junior high school he began to "hang out" with the "tough guys." As he put it, "I had all the punks in my clique. I had all the troublemakers, all the kids that would get in trouble and would go out and fight kids on the playground. I'd hang around them." Although he spent most of his time with the "punks," Alan did not engage in violence. This led me to ask him why the "punks" allowed him to "hang out" with them if he did not participate in fighting at school. He responded, "Well, I grew up with these guys. They were my friends in grade school. So we went to junior high together, and later in junior high they started to change. They started to get involved in fighting and other kinds of trouble at school, and I just kinda laid back, thinking what my father told me. I didn't do what they did but still hung out."

Alan's interaction with his parents, especially his father, seemed to have a major influence on his decisionmaking. His elementary school friends changed in junior high from practicing nonviolence to stressing violence at school, but Alan resisted this shift in conduct and refused to "go along with the crowd." Because he was a long-standing friend of these boys, they allowed him to "hang out" and remain a member of the group. In junior high "nobody ever challenged me to a fight. Nobody really tested me." Alan attributed this to his athleticism: "I'm a good athlete, always saw myself as a jock—so I was always looked up to." Alan was both a "jock" and a "punk." "It was kind of a mix. I hung around with the punks. But I was always a good athlete so I hung around the jocks too." Because of this "mix," students never dared confront him and, even if they had, he was adamantly opposed to responding with violence.

Alan was awakened to his sexuality around the seventh grade through TV, movies, sex ed class, and interaction with friends. Although he never discussed sexuality with his parents ("but I heard them doing it"), he participated in "sex talk" at school. Alan and his friends "would talk a little bit about different girls and why we liked them. Just who were the nice girls and who were the girls we wanted to be with." Alan had the same girlfriend in the seventh and eighth grades. His relationship with this girl "wasn't real heavy. It was just a kiss and tell relationship—hugging and kissing." The two would date on weekends and usually get together with other heterosexual couples—such as meeting in someone's basement—because "all my friends had girlfriends." Initially, then, Alan defined his sexuality in relation to the other boys at school.

Alan first engaged in intercourse in high school. He had one steady girlfriend throughout high school but they broke up toward the end of their senior year. "We pretty much did everything. We had sex and everything. That was my first sexual intercourse and I stayed with her throughout high school." Alan defined their relationship as "being with each other" (my term "steady" was dismissed as outdated), which was symbolized in school by his girlfriend "wearing my shirts. She'd wear my shirts to school and everyone knew that we were with each other. It got around fast." Once it had been publicly established that Alan was "with" someone, "people would ask me all the time in the locker room about sex and stuff, and I was honest with them." Although he discussed his sexuality with kids if they asked, Alan never felt the need to volunteer conversation about his sexual activity to anyone. "I didn't feel like I had to brag about it to be cool because I was already there." This comment led to the following dialogue:

Q. What do you mean "already there"?
A. I was already looked up to, so I didn't have to say "the prettiest girl came over and we went all the way last night."
Q. Were you looked up to because you were an athlete?
A. Yeah. Everybody knew me throughout the whole high school. I was known as a good athlete throughout the whole high school.
Q. You were successful in sports?
A. Yeah. When I went to high school I got away from the punks. I hung around with the jocks. I paid more attention to studies and being a good athlete. I started to become an A and B student. I played all sports. I played football in the fall, and then a week later I started to play basketball, and then right after basketball I went right to baseball. So I didn't have time to hang out with the punks—so I hung out with the jocks.
Q. What would you do when you "hung out" with the "jocks"?
A. We had a lot of parties. We'd go out, throw a party. Just do a little hanging out, mingling with friends, always drink some beer and smoke marijuana now and then.

I asked Alan what he and his friends thought about homosexuality:

> A. To me and my friends it was always negative.
>
> *Q. Were there gay kids in your school?*
>
> A. We didn't know of any that were gay but some of the jocks called some kids "fag" because of the way they looked.
>
> *Q. Did you call certain boys "fag"?*
>
> A. I never did but they would call the nerds and dorks fag. You know, the kids that paid attention in science. And the wimps who didn't go out for a team, they'd call them names. It was just somethin' they did. You know, anyone they didn't like they'd call them "fags."
>
> *Q. How did you respond to this?*
>
> A. I just let them do it 'cause they didn't call me "fag" or anything.

Although Alan felt no need to "brag" about sexuality in school, he pointed out that heterosexuality was connected to masculinity through "sex talk" by the boys. I asked for an example: "People would bring it up all the time. Like, 'how did you do last night' and then 'I did alright.' And then they would say 'you da man.' Stuff like that." Moreover, he confirmed that being seen with a girlfriend was also a masculine practice in his school. As Alan explains:

> Because I had a girlfriend, that was seen as normal—but I wasn't the top guy. The top guy went out on a lot of dates with different girls and had sex with them. It would be like, "he's the man." But if a guy had sex with a girl that wasn't very popular, that didn't make him a top guy. Having sex with a popular girl would raise a guy's status.

In addition to heterosexuality, "if you were an athlete you were masculine, and that was about it. And if you weren't an athlete then you weren't half the man that I am."

Finally, although Alan was never "really tested" or "challenged" in school by others, occasionally he would find himself in a situation that involved petty forms of taunting. When I asked him to give me an example, his response demonstrated how this "cool guy" responded during these interactions:

> A lot of people in school think that I'm the perfect kid and one kid on the football team thinks I'm stuck up, a snob. Everytime I'd walk by him

he'd just say some kind of wisecrack like, 'Oh, did you get a ride in the limo today to your car,' or somethin' like that. And I just thought he was real jealous of me. He didn't have half the stuff that I have. And he would make these wisecracks and it wouldn't bother me. He wanted it to bother me, but it wouldn't.

Q. How did you respond?

A. I just went right by him. Acted like I never heard him.

Q. Did kids call you a "wimp" for not retaliating?

A. Nah. People would just laugh at the kid, you know. I've never been called a "wimp."

Q. So violence is not something you must do to be "a man"?

A. No. I don't think beating someone up makes you a man at all. It's stupid.

Q. Why do you think you are seen as the "perfect kid"?

A. 'Cause I am. I'm one of the best athletes at school. I get good grades, and I don't get into trouble. You see, my brothers got expelled from school for fighting. So I didn't want to do that, you know. And they didn't go to college but I'm going. Maybe 'cause I'm not like them people see me that way.

Alan grew up in a nonviolent, warm, and affectionate family environment. He experienced close interaction with both parents, and he clearly cherished his mother and father. However, the traditional gender division of labor, ultimate power of his father, and remarks about "sissy" behavior created a milieu in which many aspects of hegemonic masculinity were present. Clearly, Alan had appropriated these conceptions of what it means to be "a man." Indeed, Alan was a "punk" and a "jock" in junior high, and in high school practiced exclusively the "jock" and "cool guy" forms of masculinity, which included a negative view of homosexuality and an emphasis on heterosexual and athletic performance. Alan's rejection of the "punks" was connected with his in-school upward mobility—he is now publicly a "star athlete," the "perfect kid," and heterosexual—he personifies the "appropriate" in-school masculine characteristics. Importantly, given his close attachment to his mother and father (and their emphasis on nonviolence), along with his abundance of recognition for his masculine practices in school, Alan never involved himself in physical or sexual violence. Through this interaction at home and school, Alan constructed a nonviolent form of hegemonic masculinity.

Conclusion

The nonviolent life histories show that each boy's relationship to his parents differed. Jerry experienced a nonviolent and affectionate relationship with his mother and father but since the sixth grade had lived with only one parent. Dennis suffered verbal and physical violence from his father but went on to have a loving and devoted relationship with both his mom and his "dad." And Alan lived with his nonviolent and caring biological mother and father since he was born. What all three boys experienced in common at home and school was their appropriation of a masculinity that renounced the use of physical violence to ultimately solve interpersonal problems. Although each boy constructed a different type of masculinity, what they produced in common is that the different types rejected violence as appropriate masculine practice.

At school Jerry and Dennis were often verbally abused for their physical size and shape, and for not being "a man." Yet both boys were able to discuss with their parents the unsettling masculinity situations at school. The influential adults in their life responded to their concerns, underscoring that it was wholly inappropriate for them to respond to any type of provocation with physical violence. Because Jerry and Dennis respected their parents' opinions and felt extremely close to them, they were comfortable "walking away" from the peer abuse of others—and for each of them "it worked." In addition, both boys developed close relationships with other youth who likewise reinforced and deemphasized the importance of the body to one's sense of self and eschewed the use of violence to solve interpersonal problems. Interestingly, engaging in sexuality was not a pressing "need" for either boy. Consequently, through such interactions at home and school, Jerry and Dennis then "bounced back" in a different way than the violent boys by constructing nonviolent forms of oppositional masculinity.

Alan had a different experience at school. He was never verbally abused because he was identified publicly both as a "punk" and a "jock." In junior high he even "hung out" with a group of boys who engaged in intimidation as well as physical violence. Indeed, Alan was a practicing "cool guy" who constructed this particular type of exemplary in-school masculinity in a specific way: He refrained from engaging in any type of physical violence. When advancing from elementary school to junior high, he was kept from changing and adopting violence as appropriate—as had his friends—by the crucial impact of his parents. Alan was rarely taunted, but when he was, he responded as Jerry and Dennis had—he simply "walked away" without acknowledging the verbal abuse. Involved in a variety of admired hegemonic masculine activities in school, Alan felt comfortable responding as he did because the practice never lowered his status in the hierarchies of masculinities and he was never called a "wimp" for not responding physically. Thus Alan constructed a specific type of nonviolent hegemonic masculinity.

In Chapter 6 I will compare the violent and nonviolent boys and briefly propose several social policies for curbing adolescent male violence.

6

Nonviolence and Social Change

Chapter 4 discussed why boys who engage in violence commit different types of sexual and assaultive violence, examining the movement from predisposition to violent event. Chapter 6 compares violent and nonviolent boys, focusing especially on the connections between family, school, and violence/nonviolence. Boys do not begin school with a completely assembled masculinity. Rather, they construct masculinities in social settings based on their reciprocal interactions in their families and schools. These combined interactions are crucial to understanding why some boys become violent and other boys do not. In the last section of this chapter the implications of the life history data and the social policies that can be derived from the analyses are spelled out.

Violent Versus Nonviolent Boys

As reported in Chapters 2 and 3 and as analyzed in Chapter 4, the six violent boys—Sam, John, Zack, Hugh, Perry, and Lenny—actively appropriated a physically violent predisposition as a crucial characteristic of what it means to be a "real man." The "culture of cruelty" (Kindlon and Thompson 1999) at school and conversations with influential adults at home both defined "fighting back" as *the* proper masculine response to peer abuse—such behavior representing a contextually available practice for demonstrating "manliness."

However, Jerry's life story demonstrates that an acceptance of physical violence as a means for responding to peer abuse may develop exclusively outside the home. The peer abuse Jerry experienced on the playground, as well as his interactions with others in that setting, gave rise to Jerry's conception of what the appropriate masculine means are for managing such "playground business." If Jerry chose not to bully or fight back, his masculinity would remain subordinated. Consequently, in order for him to avoid this "inferior" status he would have to "bring somebody else down." Thus for Jerry it was the playground milieu and its ongoing culture of cruelty that offered "fighting back" to provocation as a suitable resource for "doing masculinity"—a violent response to threat was defined in that setting as the contextually appropriate masculine practice for overcoming the challenge. The cultural ideals of what it meant to be a man on Jerry's playground encouraged a specific line of social action. And Jerry actively appropriated and then applied that ideal to the masculinity challenges he faced. Jerry drew on existing forms of social action to construct a particular masculinity for the specific setting of the playground. Indeed, the criteria for both hegemonic and subordinate masculinities are embedded in the recurrent playground practices whereby the relationship between these two types of masculinities are structured. Accordingly, in third grade Jerry developed a masculine project—prior to discussing the issue with his parents—that entailed responding to masculinity challenges through violence. Interaction on the playground—not at home—first predisposed Jerry toward violence, providing a resource for affirming a particular type of masculinity.

Nevertheless, Jerry's life story shows that interaction at home can neutralize previously ordained violent predispositions. Indeed, for all three nonviolent boys, interaction with parents shaped a different relationship to violence than it did for the violent boys. Jerry, Dennis, and Alan received contradictory signals. On the one hand, the culture of cruelty suggested "fighting back"; on the other hand, their parents encouraged "walking away." Thus both the home and the school offered the nonviolent boys different approaches for responding to interpersonal problems at school. The construction of both violent and nonviolent masculinities resulted from an interplay between family and school. Accordingly, let us examine more systematically the interrelations of family and school in the lives of these nine boys. We begin with a comparison of the boys who were victims of peer abuse but constructed different responses—violent (Sam, John, Zack, and Lenny) and nonviolent (Jerry and Dennis)—to that abuse.

Sam, John, Zack, and Lenny were often abused by peers at school because of their physical size and shape and for not being "a man." For these boys gender relations in school operated as a process of subordination. Each, through interaction with the culture of cruelty and with an influential adult male outside school, subsequently accepted the notion that being masculine meant responding to provocation with physical violence. Nevertheless, being physically small and/or obese in relation to the abusers, they were all unfit to respond in that particular way. In addition, all four boys were unable subsequently—for various reasons—to discuss with an adult at home their unsettling masculine situation at school. Moreover, for two of the boys (John and Zack), influential adults in their lives were physically and verbally (and for John sexually) abusive and often blamed them for the traumatic and emotionally difficult victimization and interaction at home—distance from, rather than closeness to, father was the reality. Finally, all four violent boys lacked neighborhood and school friends their age. Consequently, Sam, John, Zack, and Lenny became loners at school, in their neighborhoods, and even at home. For these four boys, the combination of school and home interaction created not only an endorsement to "fight back" but a severe lack of masculine self-esteem. Subsequently, they constructed sexually or assaultive working-class *violent subordinate masculinities* and in the process reproduced gender social structures at school.

The life histories of Jerry and Dennis are similar yet significantly different from those of the four violent boys. Like the violent boys, Jerry and Dennis were often abused by peers at school for their physical size and shape and for not being "a man." Although Jerry first responded through violence, he continued to feel insecure and "small inside." Dennis, because of his physical size and shape, was unable to respond in the "appropriate" way. Consequently, both boys felt extremely distressed over the continued peer abuse at school. However, and in contrast to the violent boys, Jerry and Dennis were able to discuss with their parents and other adults this disturbing masculine situation at school. The influential adults in their lives responded to their concerns, attempted to understand their plight, and underscored that it was wholly inappropriate for Jerry and Dennis to respond to any type of provocation with physical violence. Both boys experienced a warm and affectionate relationship with at least two adults who cared for them, demonstrated that care in supportive and harmonious ways, and never blamed them for any of the family problems they experienced at home. For example, both of Jerry's parents emphasized that their arguments and eventual divorce were caused by parental inability to work out financial problems, not by Jerry's behavior. Similarly, Dennis's mother always comforted him after his father was violent and frequently explained to him that the violence had nothing to do with

Dennis's conduct. Dennis was quite happy to see his father leave and had no desire to ever see him again. Yet his stepfather, "Dad," brought a loving, nonviolent, and supportive adult male presence into Dennis's life. This interaction with adults at home minimized the lack of masculine self-esteem developed at school. Because Jerry and Dennis had developed such close and mutually respectful relationships with the influential adults in their lives, they accepted their opinions on the appropriate response to peer abuse at school. In other words, they felt confident to "walk away." Indeed, such social action represents self-confidence rather than self-doubt.

Additionally, and once again in contrast to the four violent boys, Jerry and Dennis experienced several relationships and social circumstances at school that helped bolster their nonviolent dispositions and self-confidence developing at home. First, the method of "walking away," as both stated, "worked." When they refused to acknowledge the bully by simply ignoring his actions and going about their own business, the degrading forms of conduct seemed to diminish over time. Second, both boys developed close relationships with other youth who deemphasized the importance of the body to one's sense of masculine self-worth. These youths accepted Jerry's and Dennis's body "as is," so that hegemonic body images and practices were not essential criteria to their friends for "doing masculinity." Thus, for Jerry and Dennis, their bodies mediated and influenced their social action and directed them toward friends who accepted their bodies. Finally, Jerry's and Dennis's friends eschewed any use of violence to solve interpersonal problems—they were the "laid-back" group in school. Consequently, through such interaction at home and school, Jerry and Dennis were able to construct a *nonviolent opposition masculinity,* and their conduct challenges the gender social structures at school.

Jerry's and Dennis's life histories also differ from the *sex offenders* in an important respect. Although all five boys (Sam, John, Zack, Jerry, and Dennis) recounted their adoption of heterosexuality at school, the sex offenders developed an obsession with experiencing "sex like the guys" because this is what "every guy does." As John stated, "To be male you have to be sexual with a female." The three sex offenders did not discuss sexuality with adults, were unable to engage in heterosexual dating, and formed no friendships with girls.

The nonviolent boys' relationship to sexuality was quite different. Jerry openly discussed sexuality with his parents; he had relatives and friends who were gay; his family emphasized that it did not care what his sexual orientation was; and he had two girlfriends in junior high school. Although Jerry identified himself as heterosexual and remained a "virgin" in high school, he had numerous girl *friends* with whom he spent time; engaging in sex was not something he had to do "right now." Similarly, Dennis had numerous girl *friends* with whom he "hung out" but did not currently have an active sex life. Dennis was not bothered about not "doing it" because many of his friends were not actively involved in sexual relations either. Thus these particular forms of interaction at home *and* school that Jerry and Dennis experienced kept sexuality as a bodily masculine practice from becoming the obsession it was for Sam, John, and Zack.

The differing interplay between home and school created a setting for the social construction of violent and nonviolent masculinities. Indeed, the life stories of Sam, John, Zack, Lenny, Jerry, and Dennis show that these six boys resolved oppressive peer abuse situations at school in ways related to their differing interactions with adults at home. These interactions at home gave form and direction to the boys' practice in school (e.g., "fight back" or "walk away") and yet did not cause their ultimate violent or nonviolent social action. As these adolescents went back and forth from home to school, the practices they constructed in school were reorganized around what resulted from interaction at home; conversely, their practices at home (e.g., discussing or refusing to discuss the peer abuse) were altered based on interaction at school. The interrelatedness of home and school, and the choices made by boys during that interchange, resulted in the social construction of violent or nonviolent forms of masculinities.

Considering Alan, Hugh, and Perry, the latter two assaultive boys were analogous to the three sex offenders in the sense of appropriating a definition of masculinity through interaction at home and school that emphasized the importance of male power, the control of others, and the use of physical violence ultimately to solve interpersonal problems. They were different from the sex offenders (as well as the three nonviolent boys) in that they constructed a physical presence in school that was idolized by their classmates. When their masculinity was challenged, they physically backed down to no one, including teachers. Both Hugh and Perry constructed themselves as "tough guys" who were "superior" to "wimps" and were not afraid to physically challenge teachers' authority. Indeed, their ability to act out in class, bully those "subordinate" to them, and physically fight when provoked convinced Hugh and Perry of their own eminent masculine self-worth—they thrived in the culture of cruelty. Moreover, both boys viewed school as irrelevant to their future and emasculating to their conception of masculinity. At home they experienced emotional distance and a severe lack of "fatherly" affection from the influential male adults in their lives; school represented simply another milieu in which Hugh and Perry were browbeaten by adults. As such they joined with similar working-class boys in an unstructured, counterschool group that resisted school authority and its representatives while terrorizing and assaulting boys "subordinate" to them. Consequently, at school and on the street Hugh and Perry constructed a *violent opposition masculinity* yet simultaneously reproduced gender social structures.

Like Hugh and Perry, Alan was never seriously bullied or ridiculed in school, and in junior high he adopted both a "punk" and a "jock" presence and "hung out" with a group of boys who intimidated others and occasionally engaged in physical violence at school (e.g., fights on the playground). In junior high Alan interacted closely with these bullies, but in contrast to Hugh and Perry he refrained from engaging in any type of interpersonal violence. Indeed, when Alan finished elementary school and began junior high, he (unlike his friends) did not change to accept violence as an appropriate masculine practice. Although he continued to interact with his elementary school buddies, his close and caring relationship with his parents, and his discussions with them about violence, were crucial in deterring him from being "like the guys." Moreover, Alan received substantial respect from his friends for his athletic abilities and was never "tested" by them or others at school, so he never felt the "need" to participate in violent acts.

After Alan entered high school, he stopped interacting with the "punks" and became a "jock" exclusively. As a "star athlete" in three sports, Alan constructed an exemplary masculinity at school—he used his body in ways that were confirmed and legitimated by the school as properly masculine. Like Hugh and Perry, Alan had a body that facilitated masculine agency and he used it to successfully construct himself as a "cool guy." Yet he did so without engaging in any type of violence. Moreover, because of discussions he had with his parents about violence, as well as his masculine status in the school, when teased, Alan (like Jerry and Dennis) reacted by simply "walking away." He was never actually abused. Responding in this fashion did not lower his masculine status and he was never called a "wimp" for not physically retaliating. If anything, the teasing negatively affected the status of the teaser!

In contrast to Hugh and Perry, Alan had little need to resist the school because it was the school that consistently and sympathetically rewarded Alan for his athletic prowess, thereby offering him the possibility of a future—Alan planned to attend college on a basketball scholarship. In addition, Alan wanted to be the first child in his family to "stay out of trouble" and to go to college. Thus his conformity to the school reflected in part his desire to distinguish himself from the "failure" of his brothers and in part his bodily ability to participate in admired school activities. Given this interaction between home and school, it is not surprising that Alan constructed an *accommodating hegemonic masculinity* in school and therefore reproduced gender social structures. Indeed, by reason of his interaction at home and school, Alan accomplished masculinity through conformance to school rules and participation in school athletics, reflecting a wholehearted adoption of the school and its overall enterprise. Accordingly, Alan developed a controlled and cooperative masculine project for institutional success—he simply became an accomplice to the institutional order of the school.

In sum, the comparison of violent and nonviolent boys indicates that any conception of the "cause" of white working-class adolescent male violence has little meaning unless linked with social action. The predispositions to violence and nonviolence in the lives of these nine boys did not emanate simply from the family or the school. On the contrary, they arose from the reciprocal interplay of home and school, and from the possibilities and pressures embedded in that interplay. The choices made by each boy, and the resources available for carrying out those choices, developed in response to the specific social circumstances in which they lived. Boys do masculinity differently, depending on the social situations and the social conditions they encounter. For these reasons, then, the nine boys adopted violence or nonviolence to construct different types of masculinities.

Difference with Equality

One of the reasons for studying the differences among boys and the diversity of their masculinities is to gain some grasp as to where energy should be directed to promote social change. Consequently, in this final section of the book, I briefly address the following question: What insight do the nine lives provide us in our attempt to create social policy for curbing adolescent male violence?

Undeniably, the life histories demonstrate that we continue to live in an extraordinarily violent and sexist society; they also show how boys' practices often contribute to the reproduction of that gender inequality and violence. Nevertheless, the nine life stories also reveal that boys and their families are not monolithic in support of gender inequality and violence—three of the nine boys and their families renounced violence. These three life stories provide the opportunity to ascertain what boys— through their individual and collective practice—have to offer us in our attempt to prevent teenage violence. Consequently, what can we learn from these three nonviolent families that can direct us toward a policy to curb adolescent male violence?

Alan's life history is marginally helpful. Alan's parents never engaged in violence against each other or against their children, and the familial practice of nonviolence was clearly passed on to Alan. This shows the aftereffect—like Jerry's life story—that parent–child interaction *may* have on future adolescent male practice at school. Nevertheless, it remains unclear just how strong this parental position on nonviolence would have been had Alan not had access to all the legitimate masculine resources at school (e.g., being a "star athlete"). Moreover, would Alan's commitment to nonviolence have withstood the test of masculinity challenges at school if he had in fact experienced them? Although we will never know the answer to this and similar questions, other aspects of family practices indicated a commitment to gender inequality. Their traditional gender division of labor, father's ultimate power to control and dominate the household, and their teaching Alan not to engage in "sissy" behavior represent the endorsement and remaking of hegemonic masculinity. Moreover, Alan's individual practices (e.g., his intolerance toward homosexuality) are "complicit in the collective project of patriarchy" even though he distanced himself from the direct display of gendered power through physical violence (Connell 1995, 114–115). Because Alan is not the most suitable model for social change, we turn our attention to the other two nonviolent boys.

The life stories of Jerry and Dennis provide a starting point for understanding, in the short term, what we can do to minimize adolescent male violence. These two boys constructed alternative ways of communicating and interacting with peers. In certain aspects of their daily lives they opposed the hegemonic masculine messages prevalent at school. Jerry and Dennis, then, provide testimony that there are other and preferable paths to "doing masculinity" in school. What these two life stories point to are specific family and school practices that contradict those found in the violent boys' life histories as well as Alan's.

Unquestionably, Jerry and Dennis (and Alan) were emotionally "attached" to the influential adults in their lives. Yet the life history evidence also demonstrates that two of the violent boys (Sam and Lenny) were similarly attached to their parents, although primarily to "father." The difference between Jerry and Dennis and Sam and Lenny is the nature of that attachment—the violent boys accepted the verbalized encouragement at home to "fight back," whereas the nonviolent boys followed parental advice to "walk away." Although all four boys had, for example, caring fathers who demonstrated their solicitude in supportive ways, Sam and Lenny were nevertheless encouraged to respond to provocation with violence. Thus connection to warm and caring parents *who emphasize nonviolence* is an essential ingredient for policy on teenage violence. But we cannot stop there.

Significantly, the gender division of labor in Jerry's and Dennis's nonviolent families was considerably more egalitarian than in the violent families and in Alan's family. The nonviolent boys were offered—through interaction within the family—legitimate masculine practices that differed considerably from those found in the families of the violent boys, whose families were "doing gender" in a specific way. What this suggests, quite simply, is that to help prevent adolescent male violence we must encourage policies that not only inspire nonviolent resolution of conflicts but also democratize the family. Democratizing the family challenges the traditional gender division of labor and therefore provides the opportunity for family members to engage in practices that restructure traditional forms of masculinity and femininity. Such practices are much more likely to achieve nonviolence than violence. Shared parenting is one example of how to democratize the family.

Shared parenting challenges the traditional gender division of labor in the home by demonstrating through practice that men are just as capable as women are of nurturing children and maintaining the household. Shared parenting contributes to democratizing the household because it relieves a major burden placed on women and retards the reproduction of masculine power. Moreover, shared parenting presents opportunities for more equal relationships between women and men, allows men greater access to children as their nurturing agents, and provides opportunities for children to observe that "motherhood" is both a feminine and a masculine practice. Moreover, shared parenting encourages fathers to make active child rearing a top priority in their life—providing an example for remodeling families to challenge hegemonic masculinity.

Indeed, shared parenting helps construct what Salisbury and Jackson (1996, 278) call "good fathering," which consists of being nurturant, responsive, affectionate, and engaged with children. Good fathering permits the son, for example, to unite and reconcile opposing elements in his everyday life because it "shows a boy a world which is not a world of extremes but one in which opposite feelings and attitudes can have free play, can exist side by side and be reconciled" (p. 278). Because of the emphasis on nurturance in shared parenting, such practices can also help create a family milieu in which boys learn to solve interpersonal problems in nonviolent ways (p. 280):

> The price will be boys who can accept their vulnerability, who can express a range of emotions and learn to ask for help and support in appropriate situations. Good fathering fosters gentleness, cooperation and communication with an emphasis on finding non-violent means of solving conflicts. Finally, by accepting attitudes and behaviors which have been traditionally labeled feminine as part of themselves and necessary for full development, homophobia and misogyny will be reduced.

Both Jerry and Dennis had intimate relations with an adult male who practiced "good fathering."

To stimulate progress toward good fathering, Salisbury and Jackson (1996, 280) suggest policies that organize father groups, promote father and child workshops, and encourage fathers to attend nursery groups, enroll in child development courses, and participate in family camping projects.

Salisbury and Jackson, however, ignore good parenting by mothers. Both Jerry and Dennis had mothers who not only emphasized nonviolent resolution of conflict but were nurturant, responsive, and engaged with their sons. Such "good mothering" challenges the notion that father absence is somehow a danger to boys. For example, some criminologists such as Hirschi (1995, 135) argue that single motherhood produces a "weak family" that "causes immorality and crime." For Hirschi (p. 138), "the problem is the mother without a husband. Her children are likely to be delinquent, and she is likely to have more of them." Although having two nurturing and nonviolent parents (regardless of sexual orientation) who challenge gender inequality is good for youth of both sexes, it is *not* a necessity, since single parents are just as capable of teaching empathy and nonviolence. Indeed, Hirschi's emphasis on the *requirement* of a "husband" ignores the fact—as demonstrated in the nine lives of this study—that husbands who do not practice "good fathering" often traumatize their sons (and daughters). Such arguments help to reproduce gender inequality by disregarding the fact that many single mothers also nurture *and* lead, are loving *and* competent, and are figures of influence *and* compassion (Silverstein and Rashbaum 1994, 88). Single mothers involved in "good mothering" challenge gender stereotypes while also underscoring empathy and affection in boys.

The development of "good parenting" (whether by heterosexuals, homosexuals, or singles) is important because what boys bring to the school flows from relationships that they have with the adults in their lives. Indeed, as discussed earlier, the boy maintains an oscillating relationship with home and school, involving an ongoing interaction between parents and peers.

The problem of peer abuse in school and its emotional destructiveness is a recurring motif in most of the violent and nonviolent boys' life histories. Anne-Marie Ambert's (1997) important study of recollections of childhood peer abuse shows that the boys in the present study are not alone. Ambert found that in the 1–14 age bracket, 27 percent of respondents recall negative peer treatment that resulted in detrimental and lasting consequences for them; when calculations for a 15–18 age bracket were included, Ambert found that the percentage increased to 37 percent. Thus peer abuse at school occurs much more frequently than previously thought and has as much importance as child abuse at home. Yet peer abuse is seldom a prominent research topic, even though Ambert's (p. 106) study shows, and the present work confirms, that often the results are emotionally traumatic: "Through abusive experiences with age mates, each child victim sees his or her competence as a social actor placed in question by the abuse; his or her self-esteem is shattered, and his or her fundamental right to a safe environment is violated."

Thus a critical policy concern of the immediate future is managing the culture of cruelty and the widespread peer abuse that it produces. Indeed, abusive behavior by boys is often meant to sustain certain boys' masculine power and control in the school. Unfortunately, most schools have attempted to address the problem of peer abuse from a "personal growth standpoint" in which relations with peers are discussed as part of one's personal and social education (Salisbury and Jackson 1996). However, as

Salisbury and Jackson (p. 111) point out, such a policy is not effective unless it specifically addresses the role that violence and peer abuse in schools play as an integral part of the social construction of masculinity. Moreover, they argue that a "school policy statement" should be published and widely distributed to students, parents, teachers, and town officials that highlights that

> the school community does not tolerate the oppression of one person by another and provides an alternative ethos based on caring and valuing. Our contention is that this will be unsuccessful without concerted action that critically challenges masculinity and power within the school. There is a mismatch when schools try to create caring environments based on mutual respect and personal growth without offering work programs that ask males throughout schools to consider the way they are as boys and men. (p. 109)

One such approach that centers on masculinities and violence is the workshop for adolescent boys developed by David Denborough (1996). These workshops specifically emphasize the relationship among masculinities, encouraging boys to "find" the places and times when they and/or others do not act in accordance with a "tough guy" masculinity. Once such exceptions have been verbalized in the workshop, Denborough (p. 105) builds on these exceptions: "We ask what or who helped them to overcome the 'toughness' in that circumstance. We ask how they did it, who supported them, and how they could find further support. We are particularly interested in exploring ways in which members of the group could support one another against 'toughness.'"

Denborough reports that eventually boys describe how it requires "courage, caring intelligence, and guts" to challenge the dominant gender messages in the school. As Denborough (p. 106) puts it, "This is particularly empowering when young men articulate that it takes courage, guts, and strength to move away from 'being tough,' as these are the words and attributes deemed so necessary to traditional manhood. It is taking the old language and using it against itself."

The desired outcome of such a workshop is creating enough space for the "cool guys" and "tough guys" to "acknowledge that those boys who they hassle every day are courageous and brave for standing outside the dominant masculinity." For the "outsiders" this can be profoundly moving and empowering (p. 106). Such workshops seem to be a necessary and essential part of a formal in-school program because they explicitly support boys like Jerry and Dennis who embody alternative ways of "doing masculinity."

However, workshops on masculinities and violence are not enough; the entire school and its curriculum must be scrutinized. In a recent review of literature on "teaching the boys," Connell (1996) shows that schools are "active players" in the formation of masculinities through in-school practices that reinforce gender dichotomy: curriculum divisions, discipline systems, and sports. Moreover, Connell's overview supports the conclusion of the present study that students themselves construct hierarchies of masculinities by "normalizing" heterosexuality and rewarding certain male bodies while mocking others. Thus Connell (pp. 221–230) suggests both gender-specific and gender-relevant strategies in working with boys in schools, such as making gender relations a core subject matter in public schools (gender relevant) and creating personal development programs that are specifically designed for boys (gender specific). Both strategies have been implemented in several school systems in the United States, Great Britain, and Australia, and the description of the personal development program seems to be a beginning point for addressing masculine hierarchies and peer abuse because it consists of structured sessions on such diverse topics as developing communication skills; domestic violence; conflict resolution; gender awareness; valuing girls and "feminine" qualities; health, fitness, and sexuality; and life-relationship goals. The program is "intended to promote both gender equity and emotional support for boys, with an emphasis on being positive" (p. 222).

Finally, Connell (pp. 223–224) argues that schools should pursue an explicit goal of social justice because many masculine practices in schools perpetuate injustice—such as peer abuse—and therefore "pursuing justice in schools requires addressing the gender patterns that support these practices." Arguably, developing programs in schools that challenge division and emphasize empathy are essential. As Kindlon and Thompson (1999, 252) suggest:

There are many ways to give boys the opportunity to learn to be empathic. Tending pets is one way. Tending people and tending community is another. Boys of all ages need the chance to take care of animals, babies, the needy, older people, the environment. We see boy empathy in schools where community service programs are a regular part of the curriculum; we see boy empathy in families where brothers and sisters need care and help.

Building empathy into the curriculum enables a school to begin challenging the notion of "other" and to organize knowledge with a view toward the least advantaged in terms of gender, race, and class. Such a policy does not "abandon existing knowledge, but reconfigures it, to open up the possibilities that current social inequalities conceal" (Connell 1995, 239). For example, boys would be required to participate in curricula organized around the interests of lesbians and gays, which "demands a capacity for empathy for taking the viewpoint of the other, [and] which is systematically denied in hegemonic masculinity" (p. 240).

These suggested policies—shared parenting, good fathering and mothering, school policy statements, gender-relevant and gender-specific strategies, and emphasis on empathy and pluralism in schools—obviously neither exhaustive nor comprehensive—argue persuasively that the topic of masculinities is highly relevant to debates on the relationship among family, school, and adolescent male crime. Moreover, what these policies call for is *not* "making boys and men into girls and women"—an oxymoronic strategy—but rather attempting to make changes in the family and school that often can "reembody" boys and men by searching for "different ways of using, feeling and showing male bodies" (p. 233). Connell (p. 233) describes how such reembodiment might develop in the practice of "good fathering": "Baby work is very tactile, from getting the milk in, to wiping the shit up, to rocking a small person to sleep. To engage with this experience is to develop capacities of male bodies other than those developed in war, sport or industrial labor." Jerry and Dennis were both involved in reembodiment through their participation in the "laid back" crowd as well as "walking away." Such display and practice opposed hegemonically masculine bodily activity through its emphasis on nonviolence and the celebration of bodily difference. Thus the goal is not a simplistic androgyny in which everyone is the same, but *difference with equality*—not only between men and women and girls and boys but between men and boys as well. As Michael Kimmel (1996, 334) writes, "We must begin to imagine a world of equality in which we also embrace and celebrate difference, a world in which our manhood is based more on our willingness to enlarge the arenas so that others may enter than our ability to shore up walls and fences to keep them out."

The urgency for such a "democratic manhood," as Kimmel calls it, horrifyingly came to light as I completed writing this final chapter. On April 20, 1999, Eric Harris and Dylan Klebold entered their high school, Columbine High in Littleton, Colorado, and killed twelve students, a teacher, and themselves. Harris and Klebold allegedly were members of an outcast group—the "Trench Coat Mafia"—a label given them by the "jocks" of their high school. According to interviews with surviving Columbine students, Harris and Klebold were the objects of consistent verbal abuse by the "jocks" at school, were frequently referred to as "geeks," "nerds," and "faggots," and had bottles and cigarettes thrown at them by "jocks." As a result, the two boys allegedly often hung their heads as they walked the hallways of Columbine High to avoid making eye contact with the "jocks." On their Internet Web page they stated, "We have many enemies in our school." Moreover, five days before the "attack" Eric Harris was rejected by the Marine Corps as a recruit and allegedly was turned down by a young woman he wanted to take to the senior prom. As one student who survived the killing stated to the media, "He just put a gun to my head and started to laugh, and saying it was all because people were mean to him." Indeed, the two boys stood in complete control of the high school library and allegedly shouted, "Who's next? Who's ready to die? All the jocks stand up. We're going to kill every one of you."

Undeniably a terrifying and alarming crime, yet all too familiar and predictable to those who have read this book. In less than sixty minutes—when Harris and Klebold arbitrarily decided which students would live and which would die—these two boys were the "cool guys," the formerly subordinate was the dominant, and they were now the "real men" on campus. If "democratic manhood" is indeed a critical part of the response to this madness—and I believe it is—we can ill afford to wait another day before demanding its embrace.

References

Agnew, R. 1990. "The Origins of Delinquent Events: An Examination of Offender Accounts." *Journal of Research in Crime and Delinquency* 27 (3): 267–294.

Alder, C., and K. Polk. 1996. "Masculinity and Child Homicide." *British Journal of Criminology* 36 (3): 396–411.

Ambert, A. M. 1995. "Toward a Theory of Peer Abuse." *Sociological Studies of Children* 7: 177–205.

Ambert, A. M. 1997. *Parents, Children, and Adolescents: Interactive Relationships and Development in Context*. New York: Haworth.

Beirne, P., and J. W. Messerschmidt. 1995. *Criminology*. Fort Worth, Tex.: Harcourt Brace.

Beneke, T. 1982. *Men on Rape*. New York: St. Martins.

Bennett, J. 1981. *Oral History and Delinquency: The Rhetoric of Criminology*. Chicago: University of Chicago Press.

Bernard, T. J. 1990. "Angry Aggression Among the 'Truly Disadvantaged.'" *Criminology* 28 (1): 73–96.

Bowker, L., ed. 1998. *Masculinities and Violence*. Thousand Oaks, Calif.: Sage.

Campbell, A. 1993. *Men, Women, and Aggression*. New York: Basic Books.

Canaan, J. 1987. "A Comparative Analysis of Middle School and High School Teenage Cliques." In Gary Spindler and Laura Spindler, eds. *Interpretive Ethnography of Education*, 385–406. Hillsdale, N.J.: Lawrence Erlbaum Associates.

Canaan, J. 1998. "Is 'Doing Nothing' Just Boys' Play? Integrating Feminist and Cultural Studies Perspectives on Working-Class Young Men's Masculinity." In K. Daly and L. Maher, eds. *Criminology at the Crossroads: Feminist Readings in Crime and Justice*, 172–187. New York: Oxford University Press.

Carlen, P., and T. Jefferson. 1996. *British Journal of Criminology, Special Issue on Masculinities and Crime* 33 (6).

Clarke, R., and D. Cornish. 1985. "Modeling Offenders' Decisions: A Framework for Research and Policy." In M. Tonry and N. Morris, eds. *Crime and Justice: An Annual Review of Research*, 147–185. Chicago: University of Chicago Press.

Coleman, W. 1990. "Doing Masculinity/Doing Theory." In J. Hearn and D. H. J. Morgan, eds. *Men, Masculinities, and Social Theory*, 186–202. Cambridge, Mass.: Unwin Hyman.

Collier, R. 1998. *Masculinities, Crime, and Criminology: Men, Heterosexuality, and the Criminal(ised) Other*. Thousand Oaks, Calif.: Sage.

Collison, M. 1996. "In Search of the High: Drugs, Crime, Masculinities." *British Journal of Criminology* 36 (3): 428–444.

Connell, R. W. 1987. *Gender and Power: Society, the Person, and Sexual Politics*. Stanford, Calif.: Stanford University Press.

Connell, R. W. 1991. "Live Fast and Die Young: The Construction of Masculinity Among Young Working-Class Men on the Margin of the Labour Market." *Australian and New Zealand Journal of Sociology* 27 (2): 141–171.

Connell, R. W. 1995. *Masculinities*. Berkeley, Calif: University of California Press.

Connell, R. W. 1996. "Teaching the Boys: New Research on Masculinity and Gender Strategies for Schools." *Teachers College Record* 98 (2): 206–235.

Connell, R. W. 1998. "Bodies, Intellectuals, and World Society." Plenary address to British Sociological Association Annual Conference, Edinburgh, Scotland.

Daly, K., and M. Chesney-Lind. 1988. "Feminism and Criminology." *Justice Quarterly* 5 (4): 101–143.

Davis, G. E., and H. Leitenberg. 1987. "Adolescent Sex Offenders." *Psychological Bulletin* 101 (3): 417–427.

Decker, S. H., and B. Van Winkle. 1998. *Life in the Gang*. New York: Cambridge University Press.

Denborough, D. 1996. "Step by Step: Developing Respectful and Effective Ways of Working with Young Men to Reduce Violence." In C. McLean, M. Carey, and C. White, eds. *Men's Ways of Being*, 91–115. Boulder: Westview.

Dowsett, G. W. 1996. *Practicing Desire: Homosexual Sex in the Era of Aids*. Stanford, Calif.: Stanford University Press.

Eckert, P. 1989. *Jocks and Burnouts: Social Categories and Identity in the High School*. New York: Teachers College Press, Columbia University.

Fehrenbach, P. A., W. Smith, C. Monastersky, and R. W. Deisher. 1986. "Adolescent Sexual Offenders: Offender and Offense Characteristics." *American Journal of Orthopsychiatry* 56 (2): 225–233.

Finkelhor, D., and K. Yllo. 1985. *License to Rape: Sexual Abuse of Wives*. New York: Holt, Rinehart, and Winston.

Foley, D. E. 1990. *Learning Capitalist Culture: Deep in the Heart of Tejas*. Philadelphia: University of Pennsylvania Press.

Fracher, J., and M. S. Kimmel. 1998. "Hard Issues and Soft Spots: Counseling Men About Sexuality." In M. S. Kimmel and M. A. Messner, eds. *Men's Lives*, 455-465. Boston: Allyn and Bacon.

Giddens, A. 1976. *New Rules of Sociological Method*. New York: Basic Books.

Giddens, A. 1984. *The Constitution of Society*. Berkeley: University of California Press.

Giddens, A. 1989. "A Reply to My Critics." In David Held and John B. Thompson, eds. *Social Theory and Modern Societies: Anthony Giddens and His Critics*, 249–301. New York: Cambridge University Press.

Glassner, B., and J. Loughlin. 1987. *Drugs in Adolescent Worlds: Burnouts and Straights*. London: Macmillan.

Glueck, S., and E. Glueck. 1956. *Physique and Delinquency*. New York: Harper.

Goetting, A. 1999. *Getting Out: Life Stories of Women Who Left Abusive Men*. New York: Columbia University Press.

Gottfredson, M., and T. Hirschi. 1990. *A General Theory of Crime*. Stanford, Calif.: Stanford University Press.

Hagan, J. 1992. "The Poverty of a Classless Criminology." *Criminology* 30 (1): 1–19.

Hagedorn, J. 1998. "Frat Boys, Bossmen, Studs, and Gentlemen." In Lee H. Bowker, ed. *Masculinities and Violence*, 201–222. Thousand Oaks, Calif.: Sage.

Heimer, K. 1997. "Socioeconomic Status, Subcultural Definitions, and Violent Delinquency." *Social Forces* 75 (3): 799–833.

Heimer, K., and S. De Coster. 1999. "The Gendering of Violent Delinquency." *Criminology* 37 (2): 201–242.

Hirschi, T. 1995. "The Family." In J. Q. Wilson and J. Petersilia, eds. *Crime*, 121–140. San Francisco: Institute for Contemporary Studies.

Hochschild, A. 1989. *The Second Shift*. New York: Viking.

Holland, J., C. Ramazanoglu, and S. Sharpe 1993. *Wimp or Gladiator: Contradictions in Acquiring Masculine Sexuality*. London: Tufnell.

Holstein, J. A., and J. F. Gubrium. 1995. *The Active Interview*. Thousand Oaks, Calif.: Sage.

Hunter, A. 1993. "Same Door, Different Closet: A Heterosexual Sissy's Coming-Out Party." In S. Wilkinson and C. Kitzinger, eds. *Heterosexuality: A Feminism and Psychology Reader*, 150–168. Newbury Park, Calif.: Sage.

Kaufman, M. 1998. "The Construction of Masculinity and the Triad of Men's Violence." In M. S. Kimmel and M. A. Messner, eds. *Men's Lives*, 4–17. Boston: Allyn and Bacon.

Kendall-Tackett, K., and R. Marshall. 1998. "Sexual Victimization of Children: Incest and Child Sexual Abuse." In R. K. Bergen, ed. *Issues in Intimate Violence*, 47–63. Thousand Oaks, Calif.: Sage.

Kimmel, M. 1996. *Manhood in America: A Cultural History*. New York: Free Press.

Kindlon, D., and M. Thompson. 1999. *Raising Cain: Protecting the Emotional Life of Boys*. New York: Ballantine.

Kobrin, S. 1982. "The Uses of the Life-History Document for the Development of Delinquency Theory." In J. Snodgrass, ed. *The Jack-Roller at Seventy*, 153–165. Lexington, Mass.: Lexington Books.

LaFree, G. 1998. *Losing Legitimacy: Street Crime and the Decline of Social Institutions in America*. Boulder: Westview.

Laub, J. H., and R. J. Sampson. 1991. "The Sutherland-Glueck Debate: On the Sociology of Criminological Knowledge." *American Journal of Sociology* 96 (6): 1402–1440.

Lefkowitz, B. 1997. *Our Guys: The Glen Ridge Rape and the Secret Life of the Perfect Suburb*. Berkeley: University of California Press.

Levin, S., and J. Koenig, eds. 1983. *Why Men Rape*. London: Stag.

Levine, F. J., and K. J. Rosich. 1996. *Social Causes of Violence: Crafting a Science Agenda*. Washington, D.C.: American Sociological Association.

Luckenbill, D. F., and D. P. Doyle. 1989. "Structural Position and Violence: Developing a Cultural Explanation." *Criminology* 27 (3): 419–436.

Mac an Ghaill, M. 1994. *The Making of Men: Masculinities, Sexualities, and Schooling*. Philadelphia: Open University Press.

Martin, K. A. 1996. *Puberty, Sexuality, and the Self: Boys and Girls at Adolescence*. New York: Routledge.

Martin, P. Y., and R. A. Hummer. 1998. "Fraternities and Rape on Campus." In R. K. Bergen, ed. *Issues in Intimate Violence*, 157–167. Thousand Oaks, Calif.: Sage.

Messerschmidt, J. W. 1993. *Masculinities and Crime: Critique and Reconceptualization of Theory*. Lanham, Md.: Rowman & Littlefield.

Messerschmidt, J. W. 1997. *Crime as Structured Action: Gender, Race, Class, and Crime in the Making*. Thousand Oaks, Calif.: Sage.

Messner, M. 1992. *Power at Play: Sports and the Problem of Masculinity*. Boston: Beacon.

Miller, E. M. 1986. *Street Woman*. Philadelphia: Temple University Press.

Morgan, D. H. J. 1992. *Discovering Men*. New York: Routledge.

Naffine, N., ed. 1995. *Gender, Crime, and Feminism*. Brookfield, Vt.: Dartmouth.

Newburn, T., and E. A. Stanko, eds. 1994. *Just Boys Doing Business? Men, Masculinities, and Crime*. London: Routledge.

O'Brien, M. J. 1991. "Taking Sibling Incest Seriously." In M. Q. Patton, ed. *Family Sexual Abuse*, 75–92. Newbury Park, Calif.: Sage.

Patton, M. Q. 1990. *Qualitative Evaluation and Research Methods*. Newbury Park, Calif.: Sage.

Petersen, A. C. 1988. "Adolescent Development." *Annual Review of Psychology* 39: 583–607.

Pierce, L. H., and R. L. Pierce. 1990. "Adolescent/Sibling Incest Perpetrators." In A. L. Horton, B. L. Johnson, L. M. Roundy, and D. Williams, eds. *The Incest Perpetrator*, 99–107. Newbury Park, Calif.: Sage.

Polk, K. 1994. *When Men Kill: Scenarios of Masculine Violence*. New York: Cambridge University Press.

Pryor, D. W. 1996. *Unspeakable Acts: Why Men Sexually Abuse Children*. New York: New York University Press.

Reinhartz, S. 1992. *Feminist Methods in Social Research*. New York: Oxford University Press.

Richardson, L. 1990. *Writing Strategies: Reaching Diverse Audiences*. Newbury Park, Calif: Sage.

Ryan, G. 1997. "Sexually Abusive Youth: Defining the Population." In G. Ryan and S. Lane, eds. *Juvenile Sexual Offending: Causes, Consequences, and Correction*, 3–9. San Francisco: Jossey-Bass.

Salisbury, J., and D. Jackson. 1996. *Challenging Macho Values: Practical Ways of Working with Adolescent Boys*. Washington, D.C.: Falmer.

Sampson, R. J., and J. H. Laub. 1993. *Crime in the Making: Pathways and Turning Points Through Life*. Cambridge: Harvard University Press.

Sanday, P. R. 1990. *Fraternity Gang Rape: Sex, Brotherhood, and Privilege on Campus*. New York: New York University Press.

Schwartz, M. D., and W. S. DeKeseredy. 1997. *Sexual Assault on the College Campus: The Role of Male Peer Support*. Thousand Oaks, Calif.: Sage.

Scott, S., and D. Morgan, eds. 1993. *Body Matters: Essays on the Sociology of the Body*. Washington, D.C.: Falmer.

Scully, D. 1990. *Understanding Sexual Violence: A Study of Convicted Rapists*. Boston: Unwin Hyman.

Seidman, I. 1998. *Interviewing as Qualitative Research*. New York: Teachers College Press.

Shaw, C. 1930. *The Jack Roller*. Chicago: University of Chicago Press.

Sheldon, W. H. 1949. *Varieties of Delinquent Youth*. New York: Harper.

Shilling, C. 1993. *The Body and Social Theory*. Newbury Park, Calif.: Sage.

Short, J. F. 1982. "Life History, Autobiography, and the Life Cycle." In J. Snodgrass, ed. *The Jack-Roller at Seventy*, 135–152. Lexington, Mass.: Lexington Books.

Short, J. F. 1997. *Poverty, Ethnicity, and Violent Crime.* Boulder: Westview.

Shover, N. 1996. *Great Pretenders: Pursuits and Careers of Persistent Thieves.* Boulder: Westview.

Silverstein, O., and B. Rashbaum. 1994. *The Courage to Raise Good Men.* New York: Penguin.

Sutherland, E. H. 1937. *The Professional Thief.* Chicago: University of Chicago Press.

Swidler, A. 1986. "Culture in Action: Symbols and Strategies." *American Sociological Review* 51 (2): 273–286.

Thomas, W. I., and F. Znaniecki. [1927] 1958. *The Polish Peasant in Europe and America.* New York: Dover.

Thorne, B. 1993. *Gender Play: Girls and Boys in Schools.* New Brunswick, N.J.: Rutgers University Press.

Tittle, C. R. 1995. *Control Balance: Toward a General Theory of Deviance.* Boulder: Westview.

Turner, B. S. 1984. *The Body and Society: Explorations in Social Theory.* New York: Basil Blackwell.

Walklate, S. 1995. *Gender and Crime.* Hemel Hempstead, U.K.: Harvester Wheat-Sheaf.

West, C., and S. Fenstermaker. 1995. "Doing Difference." *Gender and Society* 9 (1): 8–37.

West, C., and D. H. Zimmerman. 1987. "Doing Gender." *Gender and Society* 1 (2): 125–151.

Willis, P. E. 1977. *Learning to Labour.* Farnborough, U.K.: Saxon House.

Wilson, J. Q., and R. J. Herrnstein. 1985. *Crime and Human Nature.* New York: Simon and Schuster.

Wood, J. 1984. "Groping Towards Sexism: Boys' Sex Talk." In Angela McRobbie and MiCalif Nava, eds. *Gender and Generation,* 54–84. London: Macmillan.

Wright, R. T., and S. Decker. 1994. *Burglars on the Job: Street Life and Residential Break-ins.* Boston: Northeastern University Press.

Wright, R. T., and S. Decker. 1997. *Armed Robbers in Action: Stickups and Street Culture.* Boston: Northeastern University Press.

Index